THE PROPHETIC

SHAWN BOLZ

Exploring the Prophetic
A 90 Day Journey of Hearing God's Voice

Copyright © 2018, Shawn Bolz

www.bolzministries.com

Special discounts are available on quantity purchases by corporations, associations, and others. Orders by US trade bookstores and wholesalers—for details, contact the author via the website above.

Unless otherwise indicated, all Scripture quotations are taken from the New American Standard Bible®, Copyright © 1960, 1962, 1963, 1968, 1971, 1972, 1973, 1975, 1977, 1995 by The Lockman Foundation Used by permission." (www.Lockman.org)

Scripture quotations marked (NIV) are taken from the Holy Bible, New International Version®, NIV®. Copyright © 1973, 1978, 1984, 2011 by Biblica, Inc.™ Used by permission of Zondervan. All rights reserved worldwide. www.zondervan.com The "NIV" and "New International Version" are trademarks registered in the United States Patent and Trademark Office by Biblica, Inc.™

First Edition, 2018
ISBN: 978-1-947165-90-8

Publisher: ICreate Productions, PO Box 50219, Studio City, CA 91614
www.bolzministries.com

Printed in the United States of America

Table of Contents

Let's take a 90-day journey together!

Growing in hearing God's voice and developing the impact of what he shows you—for yourself and the world around you—takes a deliberate journey. This devotional will help you to not only take intentional daily steps, but also to pose some deep questions only God can answer in your time with him. It will also bring you into thought-provoking connections at various points of your relationship with the Holy Spirit. As you go on a biblically based journey led by his voice, you will view yourself differently, love people more, see into the future, and understand the present and past with eyes only a friend of God could have.

I want to encourage you to give yourself over to a patient process of hearing God. To develop a sense of what he is saying takes big, risky devotional times and great intentional pursuit in a way that satisfies your heart. When you start to spend time with God this way, you will forget the process it sometimes took to get there, because hearing God will become as easy as thinking.

I love your desire to go on a devotional journey with God, and I promise that if you complete this daily devotional, you will definitely be able to track many areas of growth in your life—

even just by reading the Scriptures themselves, let alone digesting the teaching points and answering the questions. Journey, journal, and pray through this. Let your heart expand with faith until you can hear God in unimaginable ways.

How to use this:

You can use this in whatever way you want, but we designed it to be a devotional or self-discipleship tool to be done over a compacted period of time. Don't be hard on yourself if you miss a day; just do it tomorrow. Don't skip any questions, though, just because you don't want to answer them; take yourself past what is just appealing to answer and really dig deep into the tool so that you can have an outcome not even you could predict.

- Shawn Bolz

ONE

Prophetic Gifts Show the Nature of God

1 JOHN 4:7–8

"Beloved, let us love one another, for love is from God; and everyone who loves is born of God and knows God. The one who does not love does not know God, for God is love."

The prophetic gifts are supposed to first display love, acceptance, mercy, compassion, and the nature of God to whoever is receiving the prophecy. Instead, for years people have misused or mishandled the prophetic gifts as a means of finding their identity through their performance.

God's goal in talking to you is not to just be directive, corrective, or even direct. Just as parents' goals include creating identity and purpose in their children, so too God wants to reveal his nature to you and rewire your brain with Kingdom thinking and living. He wants to make your heart full and whole and help you make the best decisions you can, not make them for you. That is why Jesus spoke in parables; he was changing the perspective of everyone around him to see from heaven's culture rather than Earth's. He wanted to realign their heart attitudes and relational skill sets with those of heaven.

How have you been changed by love through the hearing of God's voice? If you are having trouble remembering, simply bring to memory a Scripture that spoke to you in love and changed you.

_____

_____

_____

_____

_____

_____

_____

_____

_____

_____

_____

_____

_____

_____

_____

_____

_____

_____

_____

_____

_____

_____

_____

TWO

Sharing Headspace with God

ROMANS 12:2
*"And do not be conformed to this world, but be
transformed by the renewing of your mind, so that
you may prove what the will of God is, that which
is good and acceptable and perfect."*

We have a spiritual mind that's intimately developed and connected through our relationship with others. As Paul says, we can literally have the mind of Christ (see 1 Corinthians 2:16). As his mind develops in us, we start to grow in our capacity to have wisdom, revelations, and profound ideas that can shape the world around us. One of the things I love about the idea of sharing headspace with God is that it renews our minds. Romans 12:1–2 talks about the renewing of our minds when we connect to God.

Continually make yourself mindful of God's thoughts. God presents us with a magnificent gift every day. He gladly offers his mind for us to connect with, partner with, and explore. As we take every thought captive and subject it to the Word of God, our minds will continue their daily transformation into the mind of God.

Pick a subject you really care about right now and sit down to really think about it. Become an observer of your own thoughts. You are in charge of what goes on in your mind. Write out all of your thoughts about this subject and analyze which thoughts partner with God and which ones seem more human driven.

_____

_____

_____

_____

_____

_____

_____

_____

_____

_____

_____

_____

_____

_____

_____

_____

_____

_____

_____

_____

_____

_____

THREE

Hearing God's Thoughts About Humanity

MATTHEW 6:10
"Your kingdom come. Your will be done, on earth as it is in heaven."

Once you start to grow in a lifestyle of hearing God, you begin to hear his thoughts about humanity. This goes much deeper than just knowing basic information about people. You start to know God in the way he wants to be known. You start to give wisdom, revelation, insight, and counsel in a way only a master strategist or counselor could. The endgame of getting to hear God is not just about giving people special words. What if God could trust us to counsel nations? What if we knew his heart about things most of humanity is dying to know about?

You are uniquely positioned in the lives around you to bring transformation and reformation unto the Kingdom because *God speaks to you.* The problems in life are daunting, but God's voice and solutions are endless. God cares about the intricacies of your day and wants to provide you with creative solutions for the betterment of your life, family, business, and all areas of influence.

Identify an area in your life where you have influence. It may be at work, at home, or with a friend. Focus on an opportunity or problem for which God's voice could bring breakthrough. Write it down. You now have a target for a specific inquiry. Ask God how you can partner with him to bring a creative solution to it. Now listen: Remember that you are just making room for him to speak. You are setting an appointment to hear him, but he is the one who sets its date and time. Sometimes it's instant and sometimes it's at a later time, but clearly inviting him in will enable you to look for his voice.

FOUR

Measure Your Fruit

MATTHEW 7:16
"You will know them by their fruits. Grapes are not gathered from thorn bushes nor figs from thistles, are they?"

Scripture is clear that if we're growing in our relationship with God, we will produce spiritual fruit. If you're trying things and don't have fruit after fifty or more tries, you need to change something. You might need a new process, a new sphere to grow in, a new delivery method, or even some personal development. In many churches you typically won't find a process or a stage-to-stage graduation like one you'd see set in place for other gifts, talents, and professions; however, you can create an atmosphere of growth by doing the following: tracking words, sharing failures, and celebrating your successes.

You alone are accountable for tracking your process in growing with God and perfecting the gifts he has provided. God desires to provide you with the fullness of Christ. In order for that to happen, and to be trusted, you must be open about the failures and successes of your journey. Trust is a byproduct of being honest and vulnerable.

Write down the last prophetic word, word of knowledge, or word of wisdom you have given to someone. If you can't think of one, then remember the last time you encouraged someone.

Let's track the words you've given. How did the word come to you? How strongly did you feel you'd heard from God? What percentage of certainty did you sense? What feedback did you receive from the receiver? Would that person want to receive another word from you?

_____

_____

_____

_____

_____

_____

_____

_____

_____

_____

_____

_____

_____

_____

_____

_____

FIVE

Every Area of Life

ROMANS 1:20

"For since the creation of the world His invisible attributes, His eternal power and divine nature, have been clearly seen, being understood through what has been made, so that they are without excuse."

For decades we have lived with this divine tension of the church being separated from politics, entertainment, psychology, and so many other areas in our culture. Now I believe God is sending us out to influence these areas, which we've had no traction or favor in for so long. I can't tell you how many Christian therapists or scientists I've met over the past ten years who are getting revelation on how to bring ingenuity and wisdom to their fields. Our faith *proves* that God is who he says he is in every arena of life.

The biblical example of this is when the devil presented Jesus with the kingdoms of the world. The devil only had those kingdoms to offer because he took them from Adam and Eve in the garden. Jesus came back to restore those kingdoms so that we could thrive in every area of life and sphere of influence, including the church, arts, government, family, business, media, and education spheres.

Which of these seven mountains (spheres of influence) do you feel called to (church, arts, government, family, business, media, and education)? I encourage you to write down and prayerfully consider the active role God would have you play, in this season, within the mountains you have selected.

_____

_____

_____

_____

_____

_____

_____

_____

_____

_____

_____

_____

_____

_____

_____

_____

_____

_____

_____

_____

SIX

Removing Performance

JEREMIAH 31:3
*"The Lord appeared to him from afar, saying,
'I have loved you with an everlasting love; therefore
I have drawn you with lovingkindness.'"*

I believe God is releasing words of knowledge in this generation as a primary form of manifesting the rest of his prophetic gifts. He wants to break through our manipulative ways, in which we use natural and spiritual information to get ahead, to help us get out of a performance mentality. In other words, God doesn't just want to tell us what to do or fill us with knowledge alone. He wants his words to communicate his love and devotion toward us: *I have loved you with an everlasting love. I know your name and you are mine. I have plans for you forever, not just in this lifetime.*

The goal of any prophecy should be to establish, reveal, invest, and communicate love. The only true way to grow in God's gifts is to communicate his heart. Moreover, re-centering our hearts to become vessels of his affection rather than performers for attention removes our carnality, because we know we freely received his gifts and should in turn freely give away their fruits.

Do you have Scriptures of affection God has given you, like Jeremiah 31:3? If so, write them out below and meditate on them. If you don't have any in mind, then search them out, take ownership of them, and read God's words as a personal love letter to you. Try to find three Scriptures of affection to claim as your own.

SEVEN

Focus of Each Word

1 PETER 4:8
*"Above all, keep fervent in your love for one another,
because love covers a multitude of sins."*

When people share words of knowledge, so many stop at high-lighting emotional needs or the need for inner healing. They stop at the spiritual conflict or brokenness they sense. These roadblocks aren't supposed to be the subject of the prophetic words you receive. Sometimes they can help build your compassion and need for boundaries. They can help lead your focus and might even be the entry point for paying attention to what God's saying inside you. But when God gives you a word for someone, these things aren't supposed to be the things you focus on. We have to show his encouraging heart.

We are encouraged to push beyond the veil of natural discernment, the need for inner healing, and visible emotional needs to provide people with the word God has presented to us. As a general rule, one should always focus on what God is doing and not on what he is not doing. If we stayed in a battle of spiritual warfare over people, they would never get an opportunity to hear what God is saying.

Help yourself grow by identifying a personal area of weakness you want to grow through. What are you currently working on with God in your life? If you can correctly identify the emotional needs you have, you will be able to differentiate between hearing them and hearing words of knowledge. Hearing God also promotes self-care and self-awareness.

--------- EIGHT ---------

Prophecy Is for Relationship

COLOSSIANS 2:2

*"That their hearts may be encouraged, having been
knit together in love, and attaining to all the wealth
that comes from the full assurance of understanding,
resulting in a true knowledge of God's mystery, that
is, Christ Himself."*

For those of us who have been around prophecy, we often think
of the prophetic as the "fixer" gift in the church. We hope to
hear something that solves our everyday problems and brings
an end to our suffering or to an injustice. Relief like this can
very well happen. After all, God is the giver of great grace we
don't deserve. But his purpose for any revelation is to bring us
closer to him. In prophecy, we see a God fighting for relationship with his children. We see a picture of Jesus finding his joy
in our pursuit of him, and who can't help but speak his thoughts
to those who will one day rule his kingdom with him.

Applying these images to the motive behind prophecy makes
us seek revelation differently than if it were just a gift with the
potential to resolve problems. There is a deeper motivation behind the prophetic that centers on a potentially life-changing
connection to God. God is a jealous God. He is jealous for our
affection, time, and connection.

Write down the names of two people with whom you want to grow in connection. Take a few minutes and write them a note of spiritual encouragement (or a prophetic word, if you get one) that is intended to grow your connection with them. Remember, it should be uplifting and cause them to feel empowered. Feel free to share it with them, if you would like.

_____

_____

_____

_____

_____

_____

_____

_____

_____

_____

_____

_____

_____

_____

_____

_____

_____

_____

_____

NINE

His Secrets

1 CORINTHIANS 2:9–13

*"'Things which eye has not seen and ear has not heard, and
which have not entered the heart of man, all that God has
prepared for those who love Him.' For to us God revealed them
through the Spirit; . . . For who among men knows the thoughts
of a man except the spirit of the man which is in him? . . . Now
we have received . . . the Spirit who is from God, so that we
may know the things freely given to us by God, which things we
also speak, not in words taught by human wisdom, but in those
taught by the Spirit, combining spiritual thoughts
with spiritual words."*

Our Father's heart for us is to disclose his secrets. Let that sink in. The creator of the universe, the sovereign Lord who says, "My ways [are] higher" (Isaiah 55:9), wants to share his concealed mysteries. I like the way Webster's Dictionary describes the word "secrets": "Kept from the knowledge of any but the initiated or privileged." We are the privileged ones. He desires for us to know his wonders. I don't know about you, but that blows my mind.

Redemption of the cross is not just in the saving of our souls but in the renewing of our minds. As we receive the heart and mind of God, his secrets about us and others will transform us to be more like Jesus. Secrets are shared and valued in trust-worthy relationships.

Can you think of a time when God shared something with you that you felt was one of his mysteries? Reflect on that time and remind yourself of what he said. If you feel as if he hasn't shared one with you, perhaps use this time to ask him what he'd like to share right now! Write it down in your journal. Always know that when you make space for true connection with him, he will always feed this place of hunger in you, even if it is at a later time.

TEN

Relationship Supersedes Rules

ISAIAH 42:9
*"Behold, the former things have come to pass,
now I declare new things; before they spring forth
I proclaim them to you."*

Words of knowledge are not dependent on your disposition, your thoughts, your understanding, or even your emotional intelligence or biblical interpretation of theology. Just as Peter said he couldn't eat unclean foods God told him to eat because it was against the rules of his faith—instead of the Lord of his faith—so too we sometimes follow our relationship with God and it actually proves the nature of the Bible we have previously misunderstood.

The Bible can only be interpreted through relationship because it requires a healthy relationship with God to live it out. As you are aware, sound-bites of information shared out of context create a false narrative. God wants us to use our living and active faith to connect with him. God has created a resource in the Bible that is suitable for everyone, all at the same time. Move beyond the rules and hard lines of Scripture into a deep and meaningful relationship with God!

*Present your belief systems to God. What do you
believe to be true about God in your own life?
Ask the Lord to bring to mind beliefs you have
about him that invite you into further
relationship with him.*

_____

_____

_____

_____

_____

_____

_____

_____

_____

_____

_____

_____

_____

_____

_____

_____

_____

_____

_____

_____

_____

ELEVEN

Knowing God

2 TIMOTHY 1:7, NIV

*"For the Spirit God gave us does not make us timid,
but gives us power, love and self-discipline."*

The prophetic brings breakthrough moments in life. It can bring tipping points. It can help simplify, or even bring solutions, to problems. But ultimately, hearing from God is about knowing and relating to him and having the faith to take risks—not just so that things go better for you or the people with whom you're sharing. Prioritizing relating to God will help you avoid the pitfalls of otherwise prioritizing his blessings.

As children of God, we shall continually put our attention on our connection to him. The blessing of the Lord comes out of a place of intimate fellowship. When we see the works of God displayed through miracles, solutions, and breakthroughs, we should be full of thanksgiving for what God has done. Furthermore, we shall see the hands or works of God and remind ourselves to look to the face of him who provided them.

Write about something specific God has done for you—a work he performed for you through a solution, breakthrough, or miracle. Now prayerfully consider how God wants to relate to you through that experience. What did you learn about him? How should you relate to him now? (Example: He helped me buy a house; he showed me a new friend; he opened up a position for me at work; etc.)

TWELVE

Our Guide

ROMANS 8:26–27

"In the same way the Spirit also helps our weakness;
for we do not know how to pray as we should, but the
Spirit Himself intercedes for us with groaning's too
deep for words; and He who searches the hearts knows
what the mind of the Spirit is, because He intercedes
for the saints according to the will of God."

Have you ever had a mentor or a really good teacher? Your knowledge wasn't the only thing that grew as a result of this person's influence. Your thinking changed. You could make better choices with clearer and more obvious outcome possibilities. When the Holy Spirit is living in you, he helps you disciple your thoughts. He enjoys seeing what his nature produces in you and what you create with it. He in no way created clones, slaves, or servants. He has always wanted partners who are free and powerful thinkers, and he guides us into fullness.

We have been gifted the most wonderful counselor, helper, and teacher. He is our personal mentor in all the ways of our lives and with God. Not only is he heaven's broker of everything in the Father's heart, but also he is our personal guide to actually transform our hearts, minds, and spirits in God. The Holy Spirit is our living and active life guide. When we let him lead, we will not be disappointed.

Remember a mentor you had, or have currently, and write down some of the qualities you admire about him or her. Have any of those qualities become part of your own thinking and behavior? Have you ever related to God the way you relate to, or have related to, your mentor?

_____

_____

_____

_____

_____

_____

_____

_____

_____

_____

_____

_____

_____

_____

_____

_____

_____

_____

_____

_____

THIRTEEN

Holy Spirit

ROMANS 8:14

"For all who are being led by the Spirit of God, these are sons of God."

The Holy Spirit releases understanding to us so that we might really know Jesus the way he wants to be known. On top of that, the more we see him, the more we understand his power and authority. He is the name above all names, the ruler over all authority. He has all power, not only now, but forever. The closer we get to him, the more we realize his authority. This has major ramifications for our lives.

Many of us were taught that God was to be feared and that he could strike us dead at any moment if we stepped out of line. But just because he can doesn't mean that's his heart or his nature. Most of the Gospel of John proves that his heart's desire is to connect with us and have the same depth of relationship with us that Jesus had and has with him. We have to have the heart quality of trust in God's ever-present love and his overarching desire to connect our hearts with his.

What are some of your primary gifts? Have you ever noticed yourself using gifts that surprised you? Are there some gifts you are discovering you operate in that maybe were gifts you didn't realize you had access to?

_____

_____

_____

_____

_____

_____

_____

_____

_____

_____

_____

_____

_____

_____

_____

_____

_____

_____

_____

_____

_____

_____

FOURTEEN

Develop an Ear
to Hear God

1 PETER 2:9

*"But you are a chosen race, a royal priesthood, a holy
nation, a people for God's own possession, so that
you may proclaim the excellencies of Him who has
called you out of darkness into His marvelous light."*

Because of Christ's sacrifice and atonement for our sins, we are
no longer separate from God, relying on prophets to share his
mind and heart. I get excited every time I think about this new
paradigm. Now we are each a priest—able, justified, and accountable to how we hear from God. Someone else's revelation
can only complement what we're personally hearing from our
creator. Revelation is not supposed to substitute for our own
responsibility to seek and obey his voice in our lives.

Truth by revelation should further our individual journeys into
the voice of God. When a revelation or truth is removed from
the active voice of God, it becomes religion within us. Religion
brings death; it is principles without relationship. When someone presents us with a revelation, we need to be good stewards
of God's voice and talk to God about it.

What does it mean to you to be a priesthood, or chosen? In your relationship with God, how do you see these principles play out in your daily life?

_____
_____
_____
_____
_____
_____
_____
_____
_____
_____
_____
_____
_____
_____
_____
_____
_____
_____
_____
_____
_____
_____
_____
_____
_____
_____

FIFTEEN

Step Past Discernment

1 SAMUEL 16:7

*"But the Lord said to Samuel, 'Do not look at his
appearance or at the height of his stature, because
I have rejected him; for God sees not as man sees, for
man looks at the outward appearance, but the Lord
looks at the heart.'"*

Here's the hard fact: In training thousands of people in the
prophetic, I have had the most difficulty empowering them to
take a step past discernment into revelation. This is the num-
ber one stumbling block to their learning to share what God
is showing them, especially among people who feel like their
spiritual calling is intercession, or anyone whose work centers
on inner healing. People are so reliant on their discernment that
many times discernment becomes the goal of their prayer lives
or counseling with others, and rightfully so in that context.

But when it comes to prophesying, discernment should always
be a tool we leverage to approach our faith in new, maturing
ways. It should be a lesser priority to us than actually hearing
the heart of God.

*Have you taken that step past discernment? If you
have, record a time when you went all the way
to the heart of God. Did it surprise you? If you've
never done this, try it this week! Now think of a
time when you didn't look past your discernment but
God did the opposite to what you thought he would,
based on what you discerned. Write that down as an
example for yourself.*

_____

_____

_____

_____

_____

_____

_____

_____

_____

_____

_____

_____

_____

_____

_____

_____

_____

_____

_____

SIXTEEN

Word of Knowledge

1 CORINTHIANS 12:8, NIV

"To one there is given through the Spirit a message of wisdom, to another a message of knowledge by means of the same Spirit."

A word of knowledge includes supernatural revelation by the Holy Spirit about something that is important to God. While not solely discerned, the information includes specific facts that will help bring God's knowledge through a manifest form into your life, or into the life of someone to whom you're ministering and sharing God's heart.

The difference between words of knowledge and prophecy is that words of knowledge can be fact checked immediately: dates, names, street address, situations, actions, etc. Words of knowledge are an illumination of intimate facts of life to bring people into an encounter with God. Words of knowledge always reference the past and present, not the future.

Are you pursuing words of knowledge in your own life? What was the last word of knowledge God gave you? Write out all of the intimate facts you presented. How many did you get right? Which facts did you already know?

_____

_____

_____

_____

_____

_____

_____

_____

_____

_____

_____

_____

_____

_____

_____

_____

_____

_____

_____

_____

_____

SEVENTEEN

Receiving a Word of Knowledge

EPHESIANS 2:10

"For we are His workmanship, created in Christ Jesus for good works, which God prepared beforehand so that we would walk in them."

A word of knowledge is supposed to make you feel as if your life has meaning. You are someone's favorite. You have a God who wants to spend forever with you. You are loved. And on top of that, you were born for a reason. You are celebrated. You can do what you were born to do. Your nature and personhood are worthy of connection. Your family is better because you're alive. Because you exist, the world is impacted and changed.

The emphasis in a word of knowledge you receive is the revelation that God sees, cares, and is actively pursuing you with a passionate, empowering love. If your experience doesn't match up with what was previously shared, then I would ask you to invite a new experience. It is safe to say that you should feel the love of God with every word of knowledge. If you don't, I would challenge if it was an actual word of knowledge.

Have you ever been given a word of knowledge?
How did it make you feel? Have you witnessed
others getting a word? How did they respond to the
word they received?

_____

_____

_____

_____

_____

_____

_____

_____

_____

_____

_____

_____

_____

_____

_____

_____

_____

_____

_____

_____

_____

_____

_____

_____

_____

EIGHTEEN

Word of Wisdom

1 CORINTHIANS 12:8

"For to one is given the word of wisdom through the Spirit, and to another the word of knowledge according to the same Spirit."

Words of wisdom are actual pieces of wisdom that come to us to help us know how to apply our plans, and even other prophetic words, to our lives. When it is a word, wisdom is like an instruction. Think of it as heaven coaching you on how to plan and pursue who you are or what you're called to, or how to love those who are part of your destiny.

Words of wisdom are revelations on what to do with what is inside us. Or they are revelations to interpret and give strategies to our spiritual perspectives, or even to other personal prophetic words. Getting words of wisdom is like having a coach or counselor explain what is going on in your heart or in your spiritual or life journey. The word of wisdom is the supernatural revelation, by the Holy Spirit, of divine purpose or counsel from the mind and will of God.

Is there something in your life for which you need strategy? Ask the Holy Spirit to speak to you about what his perspective might be on this topic! Write down what you hear or feel him saying to you.

_____

_____

_____

_____

_____

_____

_____

_____

_____

_____

_____

_____

_____

_____

_____

_____

_____

_____

_____

_____

_____

_____

_____

NINETEEN

Prophecy

1 CORINTHIANS 14:3

*"But one who prophesies speaks to men for
edification and exhortation and consolation."*

Prophecy is a word about the future that shows the plans God
has for a person, group, region, business, etc. With prophecy,
people's affections lie in the fact that God knows them and has
plans for them. Knowing God's plans and future for their lives
gives people the opportunity to partner with him to actually see
those plans fulfilled.

Prophecy is always presented with a present-future context.
Within each prophecy, people should feel empowered, edified,
and lifted up. When prophesying the heart of God to people,
they should feel as if they are in a safe place hearing words with
a positive context. Prophecy is the love language of God, and it
should be communicated accordingly.

Ask God about your own future. We all want to know what plans God has for us! Prayerfully consider the prophetic promises God has given you in your life. How are you partnering with God to bring them about?

_____

_____

_____

_____

_____

_____

_____

_____

_____

_____

_____

_____

_____

_____

_____

_____

_____

_____

_____

_____

_____

_____

TWENTY

Listening to God's Thoughts

PSALM 25:14

"The secret of the Lord is for those who fear Him,
and He will make them know His covenant."

Words of knowledge are not just about hearing God in the context of prophecy or healing. The gift of words of knowledge gives us the ability to know what's going on in the inner workings of God's mind. And when we know what's happening in God's mind and heart, we have the ability to seek his will and clarity in every aspect of our lives and world. Knowing his will can affect our families and change our businesses. It can change education; it can even reform politics.

God has thoughts and intentions toward each one of us, toward our families, toward this earth, toward governments, and toward occupations. Scripture tells us that he discloses his secrets to those he trusts. He relates information (his secrets) about other people and groups—secrets that reshape the direction of someone's life or a government's reign.

Think of something in our culture about which you would like to hear from God. Take five minutes to pray. Write down any thoughts, impressions, and feelings you get from the Holy Spirit.

_____

_____

_____

_____

_____

_____

_____

_____

_____

_____

_____

_____

_____

_____

_____

_____

_____

_____

_____

_____

_____

_____

_____

_____

_____

TWENTY ONE

Lens of Love

LUKE 19:5–10

"[Jesus] . . . looked up and said to him, 'Zacchaeus, . . . today I must stay at your house.' . . . Zacchaeus stopped and said to the Lord, 'Behold, Lord, half of my possessions I will give to the poor, and if I have defrauded anyone of anything, I will give back four times as much.' And Jesus said to him, 'Today salvation has come to this house, because he, too, is a son of Abraham. For the Son of Man has come to seek and to save that which was lost.'"

If you pursue words of knowledge, you'll realize that the gift of knowing the thoughts of God shifts the lens through which you see people and culture. Words of knowledge validate God's love for people—people others may not see in that light. In fact, getting God's knowledge actually gives you the eyes to see things you would never have even looked at without his perspective. It's like seeing another color no one knew existed.

You want to grow in authority to speak powerful words? Grow in love! Pray and fall in love with your coworkers, your neighbors, and your city, and you will have spiritual perspectives to share—words ears everywhere will want to listen to. Counting up how many of your words have impacted people is not a measure of prophetic influence. The real measure is to self-evaluate how well the spiritual love in your heart carries people so that every time you speak to them, you call them into fullness. This influence is easily felt and is measurable.

Choose a friend or family member in your life who
needs encouragement. Write down what you hear
God say about his love for that person.

_____

_____

_____

_____

_____

_____

_____

_____

_____

_____

_____

_____

_____

_____

_____

_____

_____

_____

_____

_____

_____

_____

_____

TWENTY TWO

Promises Create Peace

1 JOHN 5:4

*"For whatever is born of God overcomes the world;
and this is the victory that has overcome the
world—our faith."*

God promises to create a place of peace for those who will listen and trust in his voice, even during times of drama and hurt. His truth offers us confidence that God is with us. We can overcome because he has overcome. He went to the cross and was raised up from death, so he has already won the victory over anything we face. When you know what's in his heart, you don't have to fear what is in another's heart or the trials of this world. When you know God's heart and mind, you can overcome anything in this world.

Within God's voice you find the solutions and empowerment to bring about his promises for you. Because of his voice, you are fully equipped to succeed in any situation or circumstance. One-third of the kingdom of heaven is peace (see Romans 14:17). Peace is also your heavenly reward so that you may rest in him. God's voice should bring you overwhelming peace, even in the midst of a storm.

Think about some big decisions you are making. Ask yourself, "How am I committed to making these decisions out of a place of love and peace?" Ask God to show you where he is providing a place of peace for you at this time in your life. If there are trials, where is he providing rest?

_____
_____
_____
_____
_____
_____
_____
_____
_____
_____
_____
_____
_____
_____
_____
_____
_____
_____
_____
_____
_____
_____

TWENTY THREE

Centering God in Our Lives

ROMANS 11:36

"From Him and through Him and to Him are all things. To Him be glory forever. Amen."

God gives us revelation to reveal who he is and who we are to him. In the same way, the Father sent Jesus to the world to reveal a redemptive picture of love and restore our relationship with him. The prophetic gifts reveal God's nature, his heart, and our everlasting destiny with him. Giving or receiving words of knowledge is much more than an incentive or motivator for how we live our lives; as he becomes our main desire and focus, this gift puts God at the center of our lives.

The prophetic gifts should display a constant re-centering of God in our lives. Essentially, we shall return to our first love and see our everlasting destiny with him, with every gift displayed. God desires to show us the way he sees and experiences things. Not only will we see a fresh perspective about our lives through the gifts of the Holy Spirit, but also we will begin to partner with his perspective in everything!

What do you love most about who God is?
What has your personal testimony shown you
about God's nature?

_____
_____
_____
_____
_____
_____
_____
_____
_____
_____
_____
_____
_____
_____
_____
_____
_____
_____
_____
_____
_____
_____
_____
_____
_____
_____
_____

TWENTY FOUR

Our Minds

1 CORINTHIANS 2:16

"For who has known the mind of the Lord, that he will instruct Him? But we have the mind of Christ."

Our minds' ability to process information also acts as a proto-type to help us understand how our spirit processes informa-tion. Because we have the mind of Christ, our minds seem to intersect with his. We get downloads, impressions, or thoughts that intersect with God's huge, heavenly, loving thoughts in much the same way our smart devices receive updates to their processors.

The natural-spiritual parallels become quite clear when we look at what happens in our brains physiologically. Just as we have a neural network that our neurons, or brain energy, flow through (to create connected thought between our organs and systems), so too we have a spiritual internal network through which God's Spirit flows. Based on different life experiences and on-going education, neural pathways form when neurons fire in our brains. Neurons create pathways that grow the network of our intelligence and thoughts, connecting our conscious thoughts in more effective ways.

Inquire about something specific in your life about which you need to hear from God right now. Ask God to give you a mental picture, impression, or vision. Track your thought progression. When God speaks, sometimes he starts a new thought process you didn't create. Take some notes about the impressions you are getting.

_____

_____

_____

_____

_____

_____

_____

_____

_____

_____

_____

_____

_____

_____

_____

_____

_____

_____

TWENTY FIVE

Discerning the Counterfeit

DANIEL 2:27–28

"Daniel answered before the king and said, 'As for the mystery about which the king has inquired, neither wise men, conjurers, magicians nor diviners are able to declare it to the king. However, there is a God in heaven who reveals mysteries, and He has made known to King Nebuchadnezzar what will take place in the latter days. This was your dream and the visions in your mind while on your bed.'"

One of the most important principles we need to understand is that for every counterfeit spiritual practice, there is probably something very scriptural, something that reveals God's heart. In other words, a lot of counterfeit spiritual practices are based on something completely scriptural over which the devil wants to have power, so he manufactures his own version. The enemy is smart, yet he can't create; but he can manipulate the method God originally designed for connecting to us. You should never fear something spiritual that is not from God because, inherently, you're more empowered than the counterfeit.

Identifying the source of something is how you can spot counterfeit things. Are you being presented with a path that leads to Jesus, or to someone or something else? If you can see Jesus at the beginning, middle, and end of the road, then you are going in the right direction.

*Have you ever come in contact with a spiritual
practice that has been used outside God's original
design? How did it make you feel? We don't need to
always protest what other people are doing wrong,
but it does help us nurture the environment we are
helping to cultivate. Is there a negative spiritual
practice you have been affected by and that you want
to make sure you don't re-create in your own life?*

_____
_____
_____
_____
_____
_____
_____
_____
_____
_____
_____
_____
_____
_____
_____
_____
_____
_____
_____

TWENTY SIX

Discerning Heart

PROVERBS 16:1–3

"The plans of the heart belong to man, but the answer of the tongue is from the Lord. All the ways of a man are clean in his own sight, but the Lord weighs the motives. Commit your works to the Lord and your plans will be established."

Learning how to distinguish your desires and thoughts from God's desires and thoughts takes a discerning heart, some self-awareness, and emotional intelligence. These are essential skills, because the more you learn to connect to God's thoughts and the revelations of his heart, the more you learn to see past your own opinions and observations in life.

Within themselves, your opinions bring a restriction to the depth of relationship you can have with the people around you, because many times your opinions are set up to create a safe space or bubble for yourself rather than to create an atmosphere of love. Differentiating your own thoughts, opinions, and desires from God's will be very enlightening. You will learn a ton about yourself and about God. Consider the separation of thought as an area of opportunity rather than as a failure. God needs you to be self-aware.

Make a list of your desires. Now ask God about each one of those desires and if they match with his desires for you. Put a circle around the desires you feel are both yours and God's.

_____

_____

_____

_____

_____

_____

_____

_____

_____

_____

_____

_____

_____

_____

_____

_____

_____

_____

_____

_____

_____

_____

TWENTY SEVEN

Practice

HEBREWS 5:14

"But solid food is for the mature, who because
of practice have their senses trained to discern
good and evil."

Just as a master pianist gets a few notes wrong from time to time, so too we're going to have experiences that, even after much faith, risk, practice, and heart, just don't connect. The good news is that practice makes it so much better. When we practice, we grow in identity, confidence, security, and hope. Practice isn't about getting many more opportunities to share your spirituality; it's about learning about your spirituality and connection to God and how to make that palatable to the world around you.

The natural process of perfecting an art is equal to perfecting the ways and gifts of God. Suddenly arriving into fullness is considered the extraordinary exemption. The Bible is filled with lives lived with processes and lots of practice. Jesus even sent his own disciples back out after ministry to go and practice once more. We should as well.

*Have you practiced hearing God lately? Think of
someone who needs some encouragement and write
down everything you hear God saying for him
or her! If you'd like to share it with that person,
please do!*

TWENTY EIGHT

Desire to Be Right

PROVERBS 29:23

"A man's pride will bring him low, but a humble spirit will obtain honor."

I have learned to not super-spiritualize everything, and that has freed me from getting stuck in the details and trying to find meaning or validation for every piece of revelation I might go after. If you want to grow in this gift of words of knowledge, you must move past whatever isn't working and reevaluate your process. Seek God everywhere until you find his heart; listen to him in everything.

You also must release any pride that comes from being "right." When it comes to revelatory gifts, the need for validation, or even the need to be right, is a spiritual-growth killer. As humans, pride isn't unique, but honestly, I have seen so many people stuck in this trap and become offended when people tell them their words aren't on track. By getting stuck on their own invalidated revelation, they ruin perfectly good moments they initiate with prophetic words.

Practice some self-awareness. Are there any areas into which you feel pride has crept? The desire to be awesome? The need to be right? The know-it-all mind-set? Be real with yourself and write down a plan on how you will change this behavior or character flaw, even if it's minor.

_____

_____

_____

_____

_____

_____

_____

_____

_____

_____

_____

_____

_____

_____

_____

_____

_____

_____

_____

_____

_____

TWENTY NINE

Holy Peer Pressure

DANIEL 2:19–23

*"Then the mystery was revealed to Daniel in a night
vision. Then Daniel blessed the God of heaven; Daniel
said, 'Let the name of God be blessed forever and ever,
for wisdom and power belong to Him. It is He who
changes the times and the epochs; He removes kings
and establishes kings; He gives wisdom to wise men
and knowledge to men of understanding. It is He who
reveals the profound and hidden things; He knows
what is in the darkness, and the light dwells with Him.
To You, O God of my fathers, I give thanks and praise,
for You have given me wisdom and power; even now
You have made known to me what we requested of You,
for You have made known to us the king's matter.'"*

When the goal of revelation is to connect God's mind and
heart to the world around us, it creates a holy peer pressure to
honor people and groups (e.g., businesses, governments, and
countries) we would normally judge, either in our own human
thoughts or by our own religious convictions. I think of how
Daniel was given spiritual knowledge, yet he didn't become a
separatist from Babylonian society. Instead, he became one of
the most powerful men in the nation. He followed his relationship with God in a way that was for sure controversial to other
Jews, but in the end it saved him and his friends.

Have you found yourself judging someone, or a group of people, different from you? Ask God to show you what he loves about these people and write down what you hear. Now pick a person who is regularly in your life who is the hardest one for you to love. Ask God to show you his value for that person, as well as some of what he or she is called to do and how God wants to use the person in future, even if it's not in your life.

_____

_____

_____

_____

_____

_____

_____

_____

_____

_____

_____

_____

_____

_____

_____

_____

_____

_____

_____

THIRTY

The Gap

MATTHEW 6:33, NIV
*"But seek first the kingdom of God and his
righteousness, and all these things will be given
to you as well."*

Often prophecy exposes what God wants to do in our lives. It actually makes us aware of the gap between our desires and his. The prophetic radically matures us relationally. Words of knowledge and knowing the secrets of God are primarily for building relationship. Secondarily, they do a work through us to the world around us and demonstrate God's love to those who don't know him. We become living examples of what heaven's culture of loving empowerment looks like.

Our spiritual journey is designed by God to empower us to be more relationally mature. Knowledge from God should be a catalyst to loving the world around us. As we fill our minds and hearts with God's desires, our mindfulness changes. Prophecy brings with it an increased expectation to pull us into the life God desires for us. We need to earnestly desire prophecy!

Think about this for a minute. Are there words of promise God is giving you about your relationship with him that you cannot make happen without him? Much of our culture celebrates self-made men and women, but there are things God has called you to that you will only ever achieve through faith. Write down something you know you are called to do for which you are not qualified. By faith, ask God for the gift, talent, education, network, and skill to be given to you so that you can close the faith gap.

_____

_____

_____

_____

_____

_____

_____

_____

_____

_____

_____

_____

_____

_____

_____

_____

_____

_____

_____

THIRTY ONE

Becoming

2 CORINTHIANS 5:17
"Therefore if anyone is in Christ, he is a new creature; the old things passed away; behold, new things have come."

Jesus set the goal much higher: to *become* something, not just to overcome something. He was always focusing on the disciples—who they were instead of who they were not, despite all of the negative things he knew about them. He knew exactly what he had designed them for, and he saw them in those roles. Many times their negative traits or faults played out right in front of him, and yet Jesus didn't measure his twelve disciples by these things.

Jesus saw everyone around him just as Father God would. He knew people's potentials and constantly presented them with opportunities to step into them. Jesus always invited his disciples into a heavenly perspective, a perspective that revealed the nature and heart of God within the person at whom they were looking. Set your goal on becoming who God made you to be and bring that to the world around you.

Have you been listening to who you are not instead of who you are? Make a list of five negative things you believe about yourself. Now ask God to show you his perspective on each of those things on your list.

THIRTY TWO

God's Original Intention

EPHESIANS 1:4

*"He chose us in Him before the foundation of
the world, that we would be holy and blameless
before Him."*

God has an intention, a will, and a desire for everyone and everything he created. I love that truth. So much of his truth is out of alignment on Earth right now, but Jesus paid a price so that one day everything would realign with God's original plan. We're called to see the world the way it's supposed to be and to live with the divine tension of what it is now while standing in for God's dream over humanity.

When we can see what God's original intention was, we can bring our present world into this redeemed perspective. Just because an event took place doesn't mean it was intended and designed by God. We need to connect to God and find out his original design for our times and places and bring those about. Not only will this heal our hearts as it pertains to situations in the world, but also it will show the world the goodness of God and his redemptive nature.

Do you know what God's original design was for you? For what were you born? If you don't know, ask him to show you what that might be. Write down what you hear him say.

_____
_____
_____
_____
_____
_____
_____
_____
_____
_____
_____
_____
_____
_____
_____
_____
_____
_____
_____
_____
_____
_____

THIRTY THREE

Hearing God for Evangelism

ISAIAH 6:8

*"Then I heard the voice of the Lord, saying, 'Whom
shall I send, and who will go for Us?' Then I said,
'Here am I. Send me!'"*

When we connect with the mind of God, he begins to show us secrets in the same way he gave Paul secrets about the Athenian philosophers (see Acts 17:16–34), secrets unavailable to those not in intimate fellowship with him. We begin to feel the pull of his divine will and exchange our thoughts and ideas for higher ones that come from him. We can hear God for the world around us.

Evangelism is only effective, for both the evangelist and the receivers, when people begin to hear the voice of God. Essentially, we invite the receivers to listen to the voice of God and the Holy Spirit to speak the divine nature of God over them. We can expedite the evangelism process by asking God to reveal the secrets of his heart over them to us. Jesus used words of knowledge as a primary form of evangelism. We should too.

If you haven't already, start asking God to show you his secrets for others. What does he love about them and what was his original design for them? Choose one person in your life and ask God to tell you five things about that person you could never know in the natural.

THIRTY FOUR

Words of Knowledge for Ourselves

ROMANS 10:17

"So faith comes from hearing, and hearing by the word of Christ."

Words of knowledge don't just lead us to prophesy to other people. They are also for our own individual lives, helping us to connect to God's current and original plans for us and to bring us into alignment with his masterful purposes for us in our full identity—what I call our hardwiring. Words of knowledge strengthen our faith and restore our ability to fully walk toward his purpose, developing in us transformational thinking about the world around us.

Having the mind and heart of Christ equips us to infuse spiritual meaning and knowledge into all sectors of life, thereby assuring cultural transformation. Words of knowledge, just like any other gift from God, display a multifaceted approach to the inner workings of God in our lives. It would be safe to say that our lives would be lacking without active words of knowledge.

God cares about the intricacies of our journey. Pick a very real, hard circumstance about which you want to hear God. Ask him how he has designed breakthrough for that situation, and what he wants to teach you, as he uses even the worst things you're experiencing to work toward forming Christ in you. Write down what you hear.

_____

_____

_____

_____

_____

_____

_____

_____

_____

_____

_____

_____

_____

_____

_____

_____

_____

_____

_____

_____

_____

_____

THIRTY FIVE

Relating to Our Creator

2 PETER 1:20–21

*"But know this first of all, that no prophecy of
Scripture is a matter of one's own interpretation, for
no prophecy was ever made by an act of human will,
but men moved by the Holy Spirit spoke from God."*

Any revelation we get from God helps us relate to the Creator
and Master. He is so vast, so wonderful, so awesome, so deep,
and so beyond us. Our human minds can only conjure up so
much when we read Scripture. We need the Spirit of God to
breathe life into us and to bridge us to this God who wants to
be known by us.

The Spirit of God illuminates the thoughts and heart of God
and communicates them to us. This allows us to connect and
relate to God in ways we cannot imagine. The more we can
relate to our creator, the more we find out about ourselves. Furthermore, the more we know about ourselves, the more we love
those around us. The Holy Spirit is living and active, searching
the deep things of God on our behalf (see Hebrews 4:12). We
need the Holy Spirit!

*Have you ever heard a word, a Scripture, or a
teaching on something you'd heard many times
before, but all of a sudden you understood it in a
new way? Pick a common Scripture people use for
life application (such as Ephesians 3:20, Isaiah
60:1–3, Jeremiah 29:8, or Ezekiel 33:3) and
ask God to unlock it for you, right now, for very
real circumstances in your life. Write down the
application you get.*

_____

_____

_____

_____

_____

_____

_____

_____

_____

_____

_____

_____

_____

_____

_____

_____

_____

_____

_____

_____

THIRTY SIX

The Mind of Christ Is a Lifestyle

JOHN 15:10

*"If you keep My commandments, you will abide
in My love; just as I have kept My Father's
commandments and abide in His love."*

The Holy Spirit can help you share the same headspace as the mind of Christ and download what you could have never thought of on your own! Words of knowledge shouldn't surface in random, miraculous occurrences; instead, I encourage you to focus on this as a lifestyle of pursuing oneness with God. This gift connects you to his thoughts and the innermost depths of who he is!

There is a spiritual bridge the Holy Spirit builds in our hearts and minds to the heart and mind of God. It becomes a highway of connection, information, and fruitfulness. We see the miracles of the Old Testament and hold them in a state of biblical reverence. They were not for us to just know historical fact. We read the miracles of the past as an example of what God can do today, both in us and through us.

What can you do today, and the rest of this week, to remind yourself about this lifestyle of being present with God and about your connectedness to God? What makes you feel most connected to him? Is it music? Is it prayer? Is it nature? Write out a list of ways you would like to further your lifestyle of connection to God. Write out a plan detailing how you can take off a bite-sized piece of being present with God several times a day for the next seven days.

_____

_____

_____

_____

_____

_____

_____

_____

_____

_____

_____

_____

_____

_____

_____

_____

_____

_____

THIRTY SEVEN

God's Eternal Nature and Promise

PSALM 90:2

*"Before the mountains were born, or You gave birth
to the earth and the world, even from everlasting to
everlasting, You are God."*

When we walk with God's voice, we are not limited to our own thoughts, opinions, education, or socioeconomic status to relate to the world around us. We get God's thoughts—his expressed opinions—and we start to discover the substance of his eternal nature and promises here on Earth. God is very practical and strategic. He knows how to connect us with everything we need to fulfill his purposes in and through us.

God has unique promises for each and every person on the earth. He actively wants us to partner with the promises he has for each of us. When we surround ourselves with the voice of God, he instructs us, helps us form plans, and guides our steps. God's voice allows us to go way beyond our own limitations and enter into an eternal realm of fruitfulness. Partner with his voice!

Think about a past weakness in your life that your relationship with God has caused you to overcome. Now use the faith story in that to think about something in your life in which you still need to grow stronger or even completely change. Pray and ask God to speak to you about this issue, and give him permission to give you a plan or strategy to build his nature in that weakness or immaturity. Write down what you hear.

THIRTY EIGHT

Solutions and Life Lessons

PSALM 16:11

"You will make known to me the path of life; in
Your presence is fullness of joy; in Your right hand
there are pleasures forever."

All of us want solutions, an easier route to take that avoids the pitfalls and landmines of life. We all want the best advice for our relationships. We all want the understanding that will help us learn the most from our past experiences, good and bad. The voice of God provides both. As we focus on a life of love through Christ, there has to be a basic culture in our hearts that believes the best about his plans for us.

God thought of every possible outcome that could take place when he created us with a free will. He designed a perfect will, good will, and acceptable will of God for each and every situation and circumstance in our lives. With any misstep, his redemptive nature brings us creative solutions we need. In our relationships, God encamps around us with the solutions we need to thrive. The voice of God is living and active and ready to do life with us!

*Identify the time you felt most connected to God in
your life. Write a few thoughts about why you felt so
connected. Now write what you can do to reengage
that level of connectivity with God.*

THIRTY NINE

We Are Empowered by His Voice

PHILIPPIANS 2:3–4

*"Do nothing from selfishness or empty conceit, but
with humility of mind regard one another as more
important than yourselves; do not merely look out
for your own personal interests, but also for the
interests of others."*

As we start to understand the purposes of words of knowledge
and what they can do, we begin to get hungry for this expression of the prophetic, because it is such a relational connector
to God. Words of knowledge help us relate to people and situations in ways unique to experiencing this type of revelation. The
unrelatable becomes relatable. God is everywhere, and he wants
to bring everything into his heart.

Imagine meeting a man for the first time, but before you meet
him, you have a conversation with his lifelong friend who knows
everything about him and everything of which he has need. A
few bullet points shared can bring you a unique insight and
strategy to circumvent the relational divide of not knowing the
man. That is what God does for us. He shares his secrets with
us about the people around us, and we then become relatable.

How has a word of knowledge or connecting to
God's heart helped you relate to a person or people
group to whom you were not able to relate before?
What stands out in the word that brought
you relatability?

_____

_____

_____

_____

_____

_____

_____

_____

_____

_____

_____

_____

_____

_____

_____

_____

_____

_____

_____

_____

_____

FORTY

Spiritual Gifts Are for Everyone

1 CORINTHIANS 14:1
"Pursue love, yet desire earnestly spiritual gifts, but especially that you may prophesy."

Spiritual gifts are different from natural gifts or talents in that the gifts of the Spirit are accessible to, and can be learned by, any of us. We all have God's Spirit in us, and he makes God's gifts available to us. This means we can desire to grow in words of knowledge, pursue growth, and excel in it. Paul told us that God gave the different spiritual gifts to the body for the purpose of building up people.

At the same time, he told everyone to pursue the spiritual gifts (see 1 Corinthians 14:1). If God commands us to pursue something—so that we know we're aligned with his will—we won't fail at it. We need to desire these gifts, and our desire will create a home for them in us. When we engage in practicing each of the gifts, we begin to grow in them. The exercising of the gifts actually allows us to maintain, grow, and perfect the gifts within us.

What are some spiritual gifts you've seen others operate in that you've never thought were available to you? Write out a list of the spiritual gifts you would like to walk in. Ask God to gift them to you in a new way. How can you surround yourself with the very thing you desire?

_____

_____

_____

_____

_____

_____

_____

_____

_____

_____

_____

_____

_____

_____

_____

_____

_____

_____

_____

_____

_____

FORTY ONE

Spirit of Jesus

1 COLOSSIANS 1:15–17

"He is the image of the invisible God, the firstborn of all creation. For by Him all things were created, both in the heavens and on earth, visible and invisible, whether thrones or dominions or rulers or authorities—all things have been created through Him and for Him. He is before all things, and in Him all things hold together."

All revelation always has a source and focal point. Behind the subject and object of a revelation is always the source of the connection: the Spirit of Jesus. Everything God shows us is for the benefit of building up his Son's name in the world around us, to help establish his dominion, love, strength, and even transformation so that he can one day inherit his great reward.

This is an important perspective for pursuing the revelatory gifts. You should always prioritize Jesus as your focus. If this is the desire of your heart, you'll always have the right priority and connection to Jesus when you prophesy. When you can't find Jesus in the center of the gift, that's when you know you are using discernment to build your own agenda. What culture do you want to build in your heart?

*Write out the top five priorities of your life using
bullet points. How are you partnering with God in
each of those areas in a way that causes other people
to be impacted by his love through you? Are you
helping others, caring for your family, providing
solutions to those in need of something?*

_____
_____
_____
_____
_____
_____
_____
_____
_____
_____
_____
_____
_____
_____
_____
_____
_____
_____
_____
_____
_____

FORTY TWO

God Thrives off Our Connection

JOHN 10:30

"I [Jesus] and the Father are one."

As we draw closer to Jesus, his Spirit will come alive in us, translating the Bible for life application and good theology, and relating his thoughts for our daily lives. He can't help but speak his mysteries and inner thoughts and download them to those he loves. He is not an independent God; the Trinity, itself, proves that. He thrives off connection, and it is his joy to share with us. He wants to be known. He wants us to be one: "I in them and You in Me, that they may be perfected in unity."

We were meant to be in union with God. God will do everything in his power to bring us into full union with him—spirit, soul, and body. He is jealous about anything that separates us from this connection. God actively tries to remove anything that keeps us separated from him. We are hardwired to thrive off connection, just like God.

Think about the person to whom you are closest.
Try to define what you love the most about your
relationship with him or her. Do you have that
same kind of connection and love in your
relationship with God?

_____
_____
_____
_____
_____
_____
_____
_____
_____
_____
_____
_____
_____
_____
_____
_____
_____
_____
_____
_____
_____

FORTY THREE

Prophetic Gifts Promote Connection

COLOSSIANS 2:2

"That their hearts may be encouraged, having been knit together in love, and attaining to all the wealth that comes from the full assurance of understanding, resulting in a true knowledge of God's mystery, that is, Christ Himself."

When we speak to someone, we share our nature with that person by giving of ourselves. We open a flow of relational connection. The prophetic gifts reinforce this exchange. I love how the New Testament Gospels provide examples of how Jesus tried to connect very personally to individuals based on the Father's love for them.

Prophecy is the ability to know what is available or what is in the heart of God for the future. It is knowing what God wants to do or what he is developing someone or something to do. Prophecy makes people feel what it might feel like in heaven, as if they have some of the hope that is in eternity now. They can feel as if the rest of their life is important and worthy because they are eternal beings and because they matter to God on the most consequential levels.

Think about one of your close friends who could use encouragement. Write down five words of encouragement for that person about his or her spiritual journey with God. Try to include some prophetic perspective on the way that person is doing life, loving family, going after a calling and destiny, working hard, etc.

FORTY FOUR

You Are Your Own Prophet

HEBREWS 3:15

*"Today if you hear His voice, do not harden
your hearts."*

You're called to hear from God in a very specific way for *you*. Because Jesus lives in your heart and mind, you are your own best personal prophet. He'll confirm what he has said to you through others, but so many times it will *start* with you. Even though personal words of knowledge sometimes come from others when God has not whispered those words to you first, it's unusual for him to reveal things to you that way.

Waiting for the word of the Lord from someone else is not what we should be doing with our lives. God uses other people to confirm the things he is already doing in us. He will also use others to establish things in our lives; nevertheless, *we* now have a direct line of access to heaven. Why would we circumvent that to hear from someone other than God first? God wants to speak directly to us!

Take five minutes to prophesy over yourself about this year. What do you feel God is doing in your life, and where do you see yourself in these areas of life in the next twelve months? Get a vision for your growth and life. Write out what you hear so that you can keep it recorded and cherish the testimony.

_____

_____

_____

_____

_____

_____

_____

_____

_____

_____

_____

_____

_____

_____

_____

_____

_____

_____

_____

_____

_____

FORTY FIVE

God's Voice Brings Justice

JOB 12:22
*"He reveals mysteries from the darkness and brings
the deep darkness into light."*

God's very nature makes him a bringer of justice. God sent his Son to restore all things. God's voice helps us to see his intention, which can sometimes move things forward in radical ways. Whether it's a direct issue in someone's life, such as a death, social injustice, racial discrimination, or any other injustice or exploitation, God can share his heart about that issue in ways that can forever change a person's life. God's love and wisdom have a way of doing that.

It is not hard to find people in need of God's justice. God has a redemptive plan to bring justice where injustice resides. If you become aware of an injustice in the world, it is because you have an active role in bringing transformation to that issue. Everyone's role is different in bringing transformation, but God desires to make you the answer!

What is the main justice issue you care most about in life right now? What is a step you can take toward sowing into justice being released in that area (e.g., I care about anti-human trafficking, so I am going to financially support a nonprofit; I care about children at risk, so I am going to send books to a school in Africa; I am passionate about women's equality issues, so I am going to advocate for women's rights). Think about how God feels about this issue and ask him to show you his perspective on it.

_____
_____
_____
_____
_____
_____
_____
_____
_____
_____
_____
_____
_____
_____
_____
_____

FORTY SIX

Environment of Feedback

1 THESSALONIANS 5:11
"Therefore encourage one another and build up one another, just as you also are doing."

While you're learning something, the best way to grow is to have a clear learning process with lots of feedback. For some reason in most church cultures, growing in the prophetic has always been left up to a mystical, personal journey. The reality is that God would never give us gifts to pursue that we couldn't excel in; and to excel in anything, it must be definable and quantifiable. When we receive prophetic words, we have to create an environment of feedback and realistic evaluation.

If someone prays over you, you have every right to say you don't agree with the prayer. You never need to say it in a mean or conflict-laden way; you get to say it through encouragement. It's important you help coach the environment in which you are growing. You are not rejecting a man (or woman) if you reject his words. You get to receive him with kindness and compassion and treat him as a human being.

Have you been in an environment where you are able to get feedback from words you've given? How can you create this environment when you give words to others, wherever you go? What are three steps you can take to give and receive feedback that's full of encouragement?

_____

_____

_____

_____

_____

_____

_____

_____

_____

_____

_____

_____

_____

_____

_____

_____

_____

_____

_____

_____

_____

_____

_____

FORTY SEVEN

Developing Your Weights and Balance System

1 THESSALONIANS 2:4
*"But just as we have been approved by God to
be entrusted with the gospel, so we speak, not as
pleasing men, but God who examines our hearts."*

Developing your own internal weights and balance system is essential. In measuring what works, one would need to evaluate one's process and history. Developing your own prophetic process may take more work initially, but it will be so rewarding. You will remove yourself from guessing about effectiveness to accurately and confidently approaching your prophetic gift. You start to recognize the many sights and sounds of God's thoughts.

How is your revelation coming to you? Is it strong, and can you bank on it, or is it more of an unclear impression? Do you feel the presence of God when you get a revelation, or are you more cerebral? What ways does God currently speak to you? What is or isn't working for you personally? None of us are the same in how we relate to others, which means none of us will be the same in how we relate to God.

*Write down your answers to the questions above
and continue the dialogue with God.*

_____

_____

_____

_____

_____

_____

_____

_____

_____

_____

_____

_____

_____

_____

_____

_____

_____

_____

_____

_____

_____

_____

_____

FORTY EIGHT

Our Mental Network

1 CORINTHIANS 1:4–6

"I thank my God always concerning you for the grace of God which was given you in Christ Jesus, that in everything you were enriched in Him, in all speech and all knowledge, even as the testimony concerning Christ was confirmed in you."

Our minds are firing with God's and are being rewired with his mind. The more we develop our connection to him through the revelatory gifts, our social spiritual activity, and reading the Bible, the more our spiritual and mental neural networks get expanded and make room for more neurons and the spiritual light to travel. Don't let the word "light" scare you. I'm not talking about trying to reach a place of enlightenment in the way so many religions do. We obtain knowledge by faith in Jesus as a free gift that's already developing in us.

Returning to our first love (Jesus) in our spirits, souls, bodies, and minds increases our connection to God and, in turn, expands heaven's makeup on our lives. It may seem simple, but it is a profound lifetime journey. The more we connect with God, the greater our connection and collaboration will be with him. You, too, can increase your connection to God. We are not waiting on God to make this available to us. It's already here.

As you read today's Scripture, read it for experiential knowledge. Don't just read it to memorize. Read it slowly enough to feel what the Scripture is saying. Connect with God through the invitation he provided in this address.

What is one action you can commit to every day to get closer to God? Write it down here and practice it this week.

FORTY NINE

Making Mistakes

GALATIANS 2:20

"I have been crucified with Christ; and it is no longer I who live, but Christ lives in me; and the life which I now live in the flesh I live by faith in the Son of God, who loved me and gave Himself up for me."

Taking risks is the only way we'll grow our spiritual gifts; unless they're practiced, they can't be perfected. When we strike a wrong note while learning to play the piano, we only get the ringing of bad sound in our ears. Making a mistake while learning something that requires God's nature in order to get the hang of it often causes us to be overly cautious. God is in charge of his own reputation and entrusts us with responsibility in this, but ultimately, we can't destroy his image. It is everywhere. The whole earth is filled with him.

We need to feel the freedom to grow in our gifts. God doesn't expect us to be perfected before we practice. The process is a delight to him. Scripture speaks to the process and not just quick solutions. God provides us grace to empower us to receive a greater measure of what is available for us. Step out and be willing to fail for him. Your growth in life depends on your faith to walk in his promises.

Write down one life process you feel you are learning. Ask God for some scriptural examples that can empower you in your process. Write down what you hear and pray into it all.

FIFTY

Risk

JOSHUA 1:9

"Have I not commanded you? Be strong and courageous! Do not tremble or be dismayed, for the Lord your God is with you wherever you go."

Risk is an awkward thing because it holds no guarantees. When Olympic athletes spend years training for an event, they don't know if they'll win, but the reality is that they're still world-renowned athletes. No one can take that away from them. We're already loved by God and in relationship with him—this is enough! We get to risk the end results with what he's showing us.

I'll be the first to say that words of knowledge is one of the hardest gifts to risk with, because giving one creates a black-and-white moment. You're either right or wrong. You're dealing with absolutes. The good thing is that getting something right should never be the goal of your encounter. Your goal should be love. Words of knowledge is just one of the relational tools you're using. If that tool doesn't work, you can still pull out another tool to use to love well.

Have you taken a risk in giving words of knowledge lately? If you have, how did it go? If you haven't, is God showing you where to take a risk this week?

FIFTY ONE

Be Authentic

JOHN 17:17

"Sanctify them in the truth; Your word is truth."

When you're trying to share a word of knowledge that doesn't work out, the person will most likely question what you're trying to do and might even judge you for trying. The individual might feel you're trying to do tricky evangelism. Avoid a bait-and-switch approach; no one appreciates it. Don't dangle something in front of people to get their interest and then trick them into having a long conversation on something they don't want to hear about. All of society is wary of this approach. Our job is to be as authentic as possible and to honor people's time.

Only share what you have heard from God. Confess to the knowledge you already knew about the person. Explain how God gave you the word—seeing, thinking, feeling. Share what you believe you heard from God, not as God. You don't need to speak on God's behalf; he speaks for himself.

Do you feel you have an authentic approach when sharing a word of knowledge with people? What could make your approach more personal for them? What kinds of things can you say if you miss the word?

FIFTY TWO

You Are Not Your Gift

JOHN 15:15

"No longer do I call you slaves, for the slave does not know what his master is doing; but I have called you friends, for all things that I have heard from My Father I have made known to you."

When your identity becomes your gift, you're no longer existing. You are you; your gifts serve you—not the other way around. You don't serve your gifts. Prophetic gifts are tools to help God shine in and through you. They help you live a thriving life. Just as we see some pop-culture figures' personal lives implode because they sacrificed everything at the altar of their performance gifts, so too many people who get involved in spiritual gifts tend to get caught up in the gifts themselves, or they get engulfed in the title or entitlement they get out of the gift.

They only find joy or happiness when they perform the gift. On top of that, they stop being normal or stop contributing in all the other normal ways. Gifts bring attention that needs to have a foundation of healthy identity to maintain. Having an understanding about the core of our identity brings us into a proper perspective about the gifts and calling of God.

Do people identify with you outside your God-given gifts? If so, how? What types of attention are you receiving when walking in your gifts and callings? Journal out the steps you feel God is providing you to walk out your identity.

_____

_____

_____

_____

_____

_____

_____

_____

_____

_____

_____

_____

_____

_____

_____

_____

_____

_____

_____

_____

FIFTY THREE

There Is No Normal in God

LUKE 11:28

"Blessed are those who hear the word of God and observe it."

In our training, one of the most common questions people ask is, Is it normal if I hear this way or that way? There is no normal in God. We have no rules for how all of this works. He is the God who calls himself the Creator. Can we really define an infinite God or put his process in a box? I love how Jesus never did the same two miracles the same way. We have a God who doesn't give us scientific formulas for success in relationships; instead, he gives us tools to make our relationships successful.

This may seem counterproductive, but in giving us tools, he is actually giving us an invitation to a deep relationship. We should not be robots in our process with God. Quick solutions that avoid relationship should be cautioned greatly. We don't want to entertain an idea that removes an active God from the equation.

Write out ten one-line versions of things God has said to you about your life that were powerful. Now write down the process—if you heard those words, felt them, had impressions, or had an encounter— and see how diverse or similar the way you hear from God is each time.

_____

_____

_____

_____

_____

_____

_____

_____

_____

_____

_____

_____

_____

_____

_____

_____

_____

_____

_____

_____

_____

FIFTY FOUR

Knowing Yourself

LAMENTATIONS 3:40

"Let us examine and probe our ways, and let us return to the Lord."

Knowing your thoughts and separating them from God's thoughts is key. God speaks so much through inner dialogue. The more you know yourself in a healthy way, the more you can discern the difference between your thoughts and God's. As you mature in your identity as a Christian, you'll get to know yourself really well. This creates inner emotional intelligence, which can then manifest itself in social intelligence as well.

Our inner dialogue can also be incredibly amazing though. Our own thoughts can inspire us to ask God the biggest questions, which he desperately wants to answer. When we combine our imaginations and God's inspiration, our inner dialogues can birth great visions for what is possible; our minds can creatively think past what our own mental abilities could hope for. So much of what God says lives right next to our inner dialogue. We have to recognize the intertwining of his thoughts with our own.

This is a challenging one but it will let you examine your own thought process. Write down a list of your "God thoughts" for an entire day. Track every thought back to where it came from in your mind. How did you receive this thought? Were you reminded of something or someone? Pray over your God thoughts and ask God if he has anything further to say.

_____

_____

_____

_____

_____

_____

_____

_____

_____

_____

_____

_____

_____

_____

_____

_____

_____

_____

_____

FIFTY FIVE

Accountability for Relational Skills

JOHN 15:13
*"Greater love has no one than this, that one lay
down his life for his friends."*

Paul and the New Testament writers had no desire to separate ministerial roles from the full accountability of the core message of relationship. There was never a single role in the New Testament—such as missionary, prophet, or pastor—that was talked about more than two or three times. Our main identities, however, as sons and coinheritors with Jesus are found as a central thread throughout the New Testament. It's essential to focus on the majors instead of the minors. God is far more connected to our hearts than to our actions.

When we make the central theme of prophetic ministry or the pursuit of the prophetic our identities, it gives prophecy the same importance as every other gift of God. It's so important that we keep prophetic ministers, and people who prophesy, accountable for their relational skills, not just their prophetic words.

Write out three relational skills you desire to grow in this year. What are some steps that will help you to grow in patience, trustworthiness, empathy, reliability, etc.? Ask God to speak to you for a step that would help you grow in each of the three relational skills.

_____

_____

_____

_____

_____

_____

_____

_____

_____

_____

_____

_____

_____

_____

_____

_____

_____

_____

_____

_____

_____

FIFTY SIX

Exercise the Gifts

1 CORINTHIANS 9:24

"Do you not know that those who run in a race all run, but only one receives the prize? Run in such a way that you may win."

Pursuing spiritual gifts is much like working out. It takes practice, intentionality, discipline, and fortitude. You make it a daily discipline until it becomes second nature. The more you exercise the gifts, the more of them you'll receive. When I say I didn't start out that gifted, people repeatedly ask me if they can really grow in a significant way in words of knowledge. My answer is always a resounding *yes!*

I gave myself over to the practice and process of learning how to hear God's voice. I surrounded myself with people more gifted than I was so that I could learn, glean, and grow. When I would go out and practice, telling people what I heard from God, I wasn't right all of the time. I tried one hundred times, one thousand times, and ten thousand times. I never gave up.

Write down how many attempts you have made this year on the following things: prophetic words given; words of knowledge given; words of encouragement given (this can be as simple as encouraging someone or saying affirmations). Everyone will have drastically different results in this exercise. Create a tracking chart. Track by day, week, month, or even year.

FIFTY SEVEN

Know Your Audience

HEBREWS 5:14
"But solid food is for the mature, who because of practice have their senses trained to discern good and evil."

So many people have read the Bible, but when it comes to actually hearing a personal word of knowledge for the first time, it causes awe or shock, or even skeptical questions such as, *Did this person just research me? Is this for real?* We have to know the audience we're giving words to and really try to be sensitive to who they are and where they are in their lives and spiritual walks. That said, no one is ever "ready" to hear from God. It's such an otherworldly process!

Knowing your audience is part of giving the word. You should try to be mindful of any topics or traditions that may relationally hinder them from receiving the word. The goal in hearing God for others is to bring them a revelation of God's love. That should compel you to be sensitive and compassionate every time you give a word.

Do you remember the first time you heard from God? How did it make you feel? What was it about? How do you know you heard from him?

_____

_____

_____

_____

_____

_____

_____

_____

_____

_____

_____

_____

_____

_____

_____

_____

_____

_____

_____

_____

_____

_____

_____

FIFTY EIGHT

Faith Container

2 TIMOTHY 1:7
"For God has not given us a spirit of timidity, but of power and love and discipline."

God created you with a huge capacity to grow in faith, particularly for him to move both in your life and through you. He has given you a "container" you can fill with faith, which operates as the currency for divine interactions between you and heaven. All the best things in God require this currency of faith in him and who he is. If you fill this container, or capacity, with faith, you'll start to see more and more of God's substance manifesting in your life and in your relationships.

If you fill this container with fear, unbelief, wrong doctrine, and negativity, you won't be able to build a full measure of faith because, as a human, your capacity has a limit. There is only so much space, so you have to focus on keeping your mind on whatever is pure, right, lovely, and true—these will keep you at optimal status to be a conduit of God's heart and spiritual favor.

How much faith is your container filled with? What are three things you are doing to grow in faith for hearing God? How well are you doing at making time for these activities?

_____

_____

_____

_____

_____

_____

_____

_____

_____

_____

_____

_____

_____

_____

_____

_____

_____

_____

_____

_____

_____

_____

_____

FIFTY NINE

Lead with Blind Love

ISAIAH 6:3

"And one called out to another and said, 'Holy, Holy, Holy, is the Lord of hosts, the whole earth is full of His glory.'"

We all know this life is entirely about love, but how do we receive and share God's affection when pursuing the prophetic gifts? Our love has to become blind: we must push beyond any present negativity we perceive, discern, or have intuition about to arrive at the eternal picture—the one that shows us what God desires and longs to bring about. Sometimes we have to close our eyes to the negative and search for the revelation of what God wants in its opposite.

God is so invested in his love for humanity that his love can be seen everywhere. Not only that, but he is constantly pointing it out to everyone, trying to connect with all of humanity. He is giving us every chance we can have at the life he intended us to have. The presence of God is on the whole earth. He is so big and has so much love that his love is everywhere. We know that if he is everywhere, this loving God is constantly trying to speak and connect to humanity.

Think of a negative situation. Think through what God's desire might be in this situation, which is usually the opposite of what's going on. Release the truth, God's desire over it, and record what you hear from God. If you don't hear anything, you can still practice. (For example: You are sick but you know that was never the Father's desire, so you say, "Your desire is to heal me," and then speak healing over yourself.)

_____
_____
_____
_____
_____
_____
_____
_____
_____
_____
_____
_____
_____
_____
_____
_____
_____
_____

SIXTY

God's Original Design

PSALM 139:13–16

*"For You formed my inward parts; You wove
me in my mother's womb. . . . I am fearfully and
wonderfully made; wonderful are Your works, and
my soul knows it very well. My frame was not
hidden from You, when I was made in secret, and
skillfully wrought in the depths of the earth; Your
eyes have seen my unformed substance; and in Your
book were all written the days that were ordained
for me, when as yet there was not one of them."*

The first part of translating God is in knowing what he wants. When I pray for, say, a woman who is sick, I practice picturing her as God originally designed her to be—healthy and whole. I want my faith to have a picture, so I ask God what his original desire was. If she has a back injury and can't bend over, I picture her bending over or dancing, fully healed, because that is God's original desire for her.

It's the same with prophecy: What is God's original desire for the people for whom you are praying, and how can you give your faith a picture? Can you see them in their new jobs, moving out of state to be with family, or in thriving friendships? Take a few minutes and inquire of the Lord about a friend or a family member.

Think of someone in your life and ask God for a picture of his original desire and design for that person. Write out what you hear. Pray for the person about this, and if you feel it is something shareable, share it as well.

SIXTY ONE

Representing God

GENESIS 1:27
*"God created man in His own image, in the image
of God He created him; male and female He
created them."*

We receive deep thoughts and messages from the heart of God
that have to be interpreted. We're not just information special-
ists; we become connectors of the eternal. We learn who God
is and represent that nature, even with our words. This is far
superior to just acting as a mail carrier. We are connected to the
message. There are so many Scriptures about God's glory covering the earth or covering humanity. This word "glory" refers
to his manifest nature. It's not a power, a thing, or just his gov-
ernmental principles we get to represent; it is our God's nature!

The divine purpose for our exchange is to become transformed
just as the world around us is transformed. As we entertain the
heart of God, we should be receiving a piece of God's heart
every time. Just as we freely receive, we become ambassadors
to represent the heart and mind of God. We don't just have a
message; we become the message and we are divinely connected to it.

Read Genesis 1:27 a few times. Focus on the part where you were created in God's own image. Ask God to tell you about how you were made. Read the Scripture until it becomes an experience for you.

SIXTY TWO

Only Revelation Produces Prophetic Words

EPHESIANS 1:17–19

"I pray that the eyes of your heart may be enlightened, so that you will know what is the hope of His calling, what are the riches of the glory of His inheritance in the saints, and what is the surpassing greatness of His power toward us who believe. These are in accordance with the working of the strength of His might."

John was able to love those whom God loved on Earth in a supernatural way—he saw them in the Lord's perfection (see Revelation 19). He saw them at the end of the race fully prepared, as a bride, to meet their bridegroom and say yes with all their heart. We need revelation to not necessarily see who people are now but who they can be, and then share that revelation. Only revelation produces prophetic words. Paul wanted us all to have it and prayed "that the God of our Lord Jesus Christ, the Father of glory, may give to you a spirit of wisdom and of revelation in the knowledge of him."

We must go beyond what we can see—into a realm of faith only God provides. Only there can we grab hold of the solutions. God wants to provide us with a fresh voice every time we ask for it. He wants to be living and active within us, allowing us to see what he *is* doing and not what he is not doing.

For the next week (including right now), pay attention to the language you use while praying. Notice when it is needs based or when you use filler words that don't build true connection or intimacy. Then also notice when it feels connected and what you are doing in those moments. Plan intentionally to cut out anything that isn't relevant or that is more self-focused, and put in the things that are building connection—to make your time with God richer.

SIXTY THREE

Prophecy Is the Heart of God

1 SAMUEL 3:10

"Then the LORD came and stood and called as at other times, 'Samuel! Samuel!' And Samuel said, 'Speak, for Your servant is listening.'"

We fall in love with what God cares about because we've read it in the Word, but then we also experience his heart and fall even more in love. The prophetic is a way of communing with God. It is a culture of the heart that sees what he is doing. To know what God is doing and to bring agreement, and speak into this, is one of the most beautiful processes in which you will ever find yourself engaged.

Paul wanted to see powerful demonstrations of God's prophetic voice in every church throughout the earth: "What good will I be to you, unless I bring you some revelation or knowledge or prophecy or word of instruction?" (1 Corinthians 14:6, NIV). When you are prophesying to an individual or group, you need to let them know you are giving a directive of something God wants to do so that they will take note and pay attention to its unfolding, or until the potential has passed.

Identify three people for whom you plan to pray today with hopes of spiritually encouraging them, or even giving them prophetic words. Remember, the words need to be edifying and encouraging. Write out the words in a text or e-mail and send them to them, unless you plan to see them in person.

SIXTY FOUR

God Is Always Speaking

LUKE 19:10

"For the Son of Man has come to seek and to save
that which was lost."

God speaks and gives you hints and understanding on potentially every subject. The Bible proves he is not silent and that he wants to be known and understood. His Spirit keeps you connected to his thoughts and heart for you. As you walk with God and he speaks to you, he always talks about whom he loves and what he loves, which gives you an enlarged capacity to experience more.

God himself is the one speaking through creation, people, seasons, industries, Hollywood, and more. Many times he speaks through sources a Christian would have run from (in love). Can you look back in your life and see times when God was present when you weren't even focused on him, or may not have even been saved? That is the beautiful part of God's nature: on this side of eternity, his heart pursues us.

Can you look back on your life, especially before
salvation or in a dark time, and see when God was
present when you weren't even focused on him?
How does this make you think of God now?

_____

_____

_____

_____

_____

_____

_____

_____

_____

_____

_____

_____

_____

_____

_____

_____

_____

_____

_____

_____

_____

SIXTY FIVE

We Are Coinheritors

ROMANS 8:14

*"For all who are being led by the Spirit of God, these
are sons of God."*

Our ability to manifest spiritual fruit in the prophetic depends on our union with the Holy Spirit, not on our gifts or skill levels. Real gifts that build the Kingdom come from deep love. There will be a great distinction in the days ahead between inspired gifts (gifts that come from this abiding or resting intimacy with the Holy Spirit) and gifts or skills that operate just by the grace of how we were designed.

We will always have the tools God designed us to use, but whether these tools are connected to his power and nature or just the power of humanity is up to us. Sometimes even church people have no identity in God but they can still be gifted. God has given all of humanity access to its full, uniquely designed, eternal tool set, but we can't minister these gifts with all of heaven's worth, life, and fulfillment without relationship with the Father.

What has God spoken to your eternal identity of sonship and being an heir? What Scriptures touch you about this theme? How does that change the way you relate to your life? Have you let that significance touch you every day?

_____

_____

_____

_____

_____

_____

_____

_____

_____

_____

_____

_____

_____

_____

_____

_____

_____

_____

_____

_____

_____

_____

_____

_____

SIXTY SIX

Self-Accountability

GALATIANS 6:9

*"Let us not lose heart in doing good, for in due time
we will reap if we do not grow weary."*

Part of growing is the ability to track change and progress as
well as mistakes. For the times you are growing in the prophetic, I want to invite you to an accountability process that
hopefully will last throughout your pursuit of prophetic gifts.
If you are going to grow with intention, you need to be able to
measure your growth. That means checking in to see how much
your words connected with those to whom you gave words,
how accurate the words were, if your specific prophecies actually happened, if your words of knowledge were on target, and if
your words of wisdom were helpful or useful.

Learning to weigh the presentation, the heart, the anointing,
and the communication skill level can be daunting unless you
take a relational approach to it all. This can be more of an ar-
tistic process at times than a direct science, because it involves
communication about the heart of God. Weighing your words
will cause you to grow.

Where do you feel like you've grown in the prophetic in the past few months? What areas have been difficult for you? What are some areas in which you have had some great wins?

_____
_____
_____
_____
_____
_____
_____
_____
_____
_____
_____
_____
_____
_____
_____
_____
_____
_____
_____
_____
_____
_____
_____
_____
_____

SIXTY SEVEN

Practice Skill Building

PHILIPPIANS 4:9
"The things you have learned and received and heard and seen in me, practice these things, and the God of peace will be with you."

For some reason, many people think prophets should be able to bypass the practice and skill-building process of moving in the prophetic. Can you imagine listening to any mature, well-known speaker first starting out? It takes hundreds, if not thousands, of attempts at public speaking and teaching before you become decent and relatable, and that is if you are doing it in an educated way. For some reason, we expect people to prophesy as experts in their first seasons of trial and error, but it just never happens that way.

People should have individual paths of pursuit to perfect their own skills, and not just spiritual skills but emotional and social skills, such as the abilities of being more relational, communicative, and self-aware. Have you considered working on becoming a better public speaker if you desire to talk in public? There are tons of audio books, online courses, books, and classes to help you become more skilled.

Reflect on something else you've had to practice a lot to get good at. How was that process for you? When it comes to words of knowledge, how does this skill-building process apply to you personally? What areas need the most practice? Maybe it's moving past discernment. Maybe it's taking the risk in the first place. Maybe it's following up with the person after you've given a word. What has been the easiest or best thing?

———— SIXTY EIGHT ————

Risk-Taking

ISAIAH 64:8

*"But now, O Lord, You are our Father, we are the
clay, and You our potter; and all of us are the work
of Your hand."*

Be emotionally intelligent and understand your environment,
but by all means try new things. God's imagination is huge and
will inspire you to do things you would have never thought of.
That is one of the purest indicators I have of when a thought is
God's—it's something I would have never thought of, and it's
not just a repeat of the last thing I did. God is so exciting and
creative. He uses the prophetic to create images and snapshots
of his love that we will re-watch in heaven more often than kids
watch reruns of their favorite cartoons.

As you continue your journey in stepping out in faith, consider
the reward set before Jesus and why he endured the cross. This
will cause you to have elevated faith to help you take those steps
of faith. Step out to grow; step out for him.

How does God want you to be creative in your journey? As you grow in the prophetic, ask him how you can partner with him in creativity. Ask him to give you creative inspiration.

_____
_____
_____
_____
_____
_____
_____
_____
_____
_____
_____
_____
_____
_____
_____
_____
_____
_____
_____
_____
_____
_____
_____
_____
_____
_____

SIXTY NINE

Beware of Patterns

EPHESIANS 3:20
"Now to Him who is able to do far more abundantly beyond all that we ask or think, according to the power that works within us."

I see spiritual boredom come when people try to re-create their success over and over by only hearing God one way or doing things a set way. The problem with this is, for example, that you might see that a guy's favorite color is blue and interpret that he is going to grow in revelation, but the next time you see the color blue for a guy, it may not mean the same thing.

Maybe it was the color he just painted his room and God wants to show him how much he loves his love for the color blue because it was his father's favorite color—and his dad died but is now in eternity. These are both examples of words I have received. If you get stuck thinking you can do rote interpretations, you might miss the nuances of God's great and extravagant creative love.

Can you identify your default patterns? What kinds of ways do you usually hear God? What kinds of words do you find yourself giving to people? How can you look for ways God can change up some of your regular ways of interacting in the prophetic? (I give a lot of words about family and marriage, and I often find I end up asking God about these things as my default, because I am so passionate about them.) What areas does God want to focus you on that are not on your grid but they are on his?

SEVENTY

Ask Lots of Questions

LUKE 12:2

"But there is nothing covered up that will not be revealed, and hidden that will not be known."

If you aren't getting revelation, don't just think God isn't talking. He loves to hide himself so that you can come find him. He loves the chase and the intimacy it builds. If I hear nothing and I am praying about a male friend, I ask God the following five things: (1) What do you love about this person most right now? (2) What do you want to say about his relationships and/ or friendships? What are you doing there?

(3) What is he spending his time on? Is it in a job or career or hobby you love, God? (4) What is his spiritual calling? (5) What are good secrets that would reveal your God nature to him? Notice that I start with the love of God and the person's heart. The old prophetic movement always started with a person's calling, which is really not where the prophetic should usually start. God is always a connector of heart before purpose.

Think of a person and ask God the above questions about the individual. Just keep asking questions!

_____
_____
_____
_____
_____
_____
_____
_____
_____
_____
_____
_____
_____
_____
_____
_____
_____
_____
_____
_____
_____
_____
_____
_____
_____

SEVENTY ONE

The Prophetic Accelerates Relationship

1 JOHN 4:7

"Beloved, let us love one another, for love is from God; and everyone who loves is born of God and knows God."

The prophetic is like the technology or smart device to our spiritual love. It is the tool that accelerates relationship and creates connection with people, cities, countries, industries, and the world. As with technology, revelation was not just meant to inspire prophetic gifts but to help us live with a connection to how God feels and what he thinks as part of our way of life. He wants us to see people the way he's always longed for them to be seen and, from that revelation, to treat them out of his culture of love so that they will want to be the version of themselves we see.

We get to do that! When people see who God is and what he wants, and if they want to be connected to God, they will protect that connection at all costs once they experience it. However, if we start out not giving a revelation of who God is but only giving the principles of his kingdom, then people will never come into (or want to come into) a place of relationship with him.

*Ask God to show you three people with whom
to spend time this week or month. Ask the Holy
Spirit to speak to you in ways that would help you
understand them even before you get to know them.
Invite them out for a coffee to specifically hear about
their spiritual journey. Enjoy the prophetic skill of
listening well without commenting or preaching but
practicing empathy, understanding, and compassion.
See what kind of relational chemistry God gives you
when you allow him the space to move.*

SEVENTY TWO

See What God Sees

JOHN 17:24

"Father, I desire that they also, whom You have given Me, be with Me where I am, so that they may see My glory which You have given Me, for You loved Me before the foundation of the world."

The goal of revelation is so simple: See what God sees, hear what God hears, and speak what God speaks so that we can all love the way God loves. Revelation is given to us so that we can carry a piece of God's heart from eternity into the world. "We prophesy each time we make known his passionate heart" (Mike Bickle).

When Jesus was moved by compassion, it was not just a feeling he had but an understanding and conviction of what those people meant to the Father. Their value in the eternal realm was not just based on their immediate healings; Jesus could see what would happen if they had a connection again to God, if they could walk in the fullness of the purposes for which they were created. He also saw them as though they were already eternal, and he pulled them into that place just by loving them. Ultimately, he laid down his life to reconnect them to the Father because he believed in the value of that connection.

*Write out several things you know God is currently
doing in your life. Ask God for a fresh perspective
and a fresh word about them. What does God want
to say about these things today?*

SEVENTY THREE

Win the Prize

PHILIPPIANS 3:12–14

*"Not that I have already obtained it or have already
become perfect, but I press on so that I may lay hold of that
for which also I was laid hold of by Christ Jesus. Brethren,
I do not regard myself as having laid hold of it yet; but
one thing I do: forgetting what lies behind and reaching
forward to what lies ahead, I press on toward the goal for
the prize of the upward call of God in Christ Jesus."*

Paul talked about sports and running races quite a few times. Running a race is such a great picture of the Christian journey, and one essential to have in your perspective when you think about prophecy, because it will help set the goal higher for you. Paul talked about every believer needing to run as though he were going to get the gold, because a runner doesn't run the race to get the silver or bronze. He runs for the gold. When John came back from heaven, he had new eyes of revelation. He began to treat every man as if he had already won the race set before him.

Your goal in giving revelation to others should be to encourage them that they aren't just good runners in a race, but that they are worthy of the first-place prize. Revelation empowers you to see everyone around you as a winner, as the bride ready for the wedding feast. It also helps you to see how to help people and groups overcome obstacles that would keep them from empowerment.

Pick a person or two in your life with whom you are experiencing some challenges. Ask God to show you them in fullness. What would they look like if they were operating out of their full capacity of love, talents, gifts, relational skills, and grace? Pray that God would encounter them. See them at the end of the race with trophies in their hands for their character, life goals, personality, and more.

SEVENTY FOUR

Love Is the Main Goal

1 CORINTHIANS 13:1

*"If I speak with the tongues of men and of angels,
but do not have love, I have become a noisy gong or
a clanging cymbal."*

Paul encourages the Corinthians to follow the way of love or pursue love as the main goal, but also to eagerly desire spiritual gifts, and he highlights the gift of prophecy (see 1 Corinthians 14:1). The reason is because prophecy can be one of the clearest validations of the Father's great love, for which Jesus paid such a high price. When people hear the thoughts and emotions of God toward them, they believe in his love for them.

There is no power from God separated from love. If you want to have influence, you have to join yourself to his love nature. This is more than a feeling or an emotion. It is an attitude of acceptance toward everyone and everything that is God's, even if you can't control it, manage it, or even nurture it. You are called to see everyone before you as if he or she has already become healed and whole. You are called to love.

Think of the last important conversation you had.
How could you have made that conversation more
about love—loving the person or the topic at hand?
At the end of the day, it's all about love. Write out
what you become mindful of when you look for
love at the center of your interactions. Ask God
to help you.

SEVENTY FIVE

Participating with His Nature

2 CORINTHIANS 12:9

"And He has said to me, 'My grace is sufficient for you, for power is perfected in weakness.' Most gladly, therefore, I will rather boast about my weaknesses, so that the power of Christ may dwell in me."

We cannot limit ourselves or our understanding of God. Participating with his nature means we are not limited to our weaknesses or strengths, our personality, our gifts, our talents, or our emotions. We have a living God who also has all of these strengths we relate to. The nature of the supernatural does not depend on the nature, skills, gifts, or callings of man but on the actual supernatural love of God imparted to us, the vessels of his honor.

When you are partnering with this nature, you will make decisions that don't always seem like yours. You will go places and talk to people and do things that are not limited to your rational thinking or your life experiences. You will also do things out of his goodness and have an instinct for what will make the world better. You will be more willing to move on faith than react in fear.

Think about one circumstance or issue that causes you anxiety or fear (e.g., politics, health, finances, relationships). Try to diagnose what causes you anxiety and then ask God to change your heart and see his strength in it. What did he show you?

SEVENTY SIX

Prophecy Should Never Violate Our Ability to Have Choices

HEBREWS 4:12

"For the word of God is living and active and sharper than any two-edged sword, and piercing as far as the division of soul and spirit, of both joints and marrow, and able to judge the thoughts and intentions of the heart."

Prophecy should be encouraging, comforting, and edifying because God is already speaking in our core being; and prophecy should validate what we already know about empowering others through love. It doesn't mean our prophetic words won't have new direction or connection, but prophecy isn't supposed to have the goal of being directive in a commanding way. It should leave room for the persons receiving the word to be accountable to God themselves for their choices, not demanding this choice be made for them.

If you think God has spoken and you use what you hear to direct and lead people in ways they wouldn't normally go, you are violating their own faith journeys with God. The world doesn't need another Holy Spirit or another Jesus; it needs the connection to the One it already has. Any man (or woman) trying to substitute himself into this role will find himself to be a very legalistic and unfulfilling leader.

Write out the last prophetic word, word of knowledge, or piece of advice you gave a woman (or man). Now ask yourself these questions: Did she have the freedom to choose not to receive your word? Did you tell her the word "was" from God or it "might be" from God? Did you ask her how she felt after? Did you give directional statements or advice? How did you connect her with the Holy Spirit?

_____

_____

_____

_____

_____

_____

_____

_____

_____

_____

_____

_____

_____

_____

_____

_____

_____

_____

SEVENTY SEVEN

Discernment Is a Conversation Starter

PHILIPPIANS 1:9–10

"And this I pray, that your love may abound still more and more in real knowledge and all discernment, so that you may approve the things that are excellent, in order to be sincere and blameless until the day of Christ."

When you discern things, you're not necessarily getting a prophetic message of revelation. It's more of a conversation starter. It's God helping your spirit man use your spiritual eyes and feelings to know and glimpse the world around you. It's all the senses plus your spiritual senses working together, and they are God's gifts of connection to you. Connect with God first and allow your discernment to be the door for spiritual revelation that goes beyond your thoughts, feelings, opinions, or faith. Take what you discern and talk to him about it. Then he can reveal his deep heart and share his thoughts about it.

God has given you discernment so that you can pray and get *his* spiritual perspective. Sometimes God shows you what is not happening so that you can define the void and pray a resolution from his heart. Sometimes he shows you what people are not doing so that you can hear God's heart about what he wants to raise up. For everything you discern, there is a deeper, more original thought about it in God's heart.

Do you feel as if you've taken that step past discernment into God's spiritual perspective? Ask God how he can take you there and show you how to pray past discernment. Ask him to show you what is in his thoughts and mind in the first place. (This takes you past even true negative facts about the person and into a fuller picture of who he or she is.)

_____

_____

_____

_____

_____

_____

_____

_____

_____

_____

_____

_____

_____

_____

_____

_____

_____

_____

_____

_____

SEVENTY EIGHT

Shake It Off

PSALM 32:8

"I will instruct you and teach you in the way which you should go; I will counsel you with My eye upon you."

You need to be real with the people you love. If they are praying something you don't appreciate, set them straight so that they're on the right track in their prayer for you. If some people don't know you and prophesy something that doesn't feel like it's from God's heart, shake it off! They aren't your ultimate authorities; they are just believers trying to get closer to God's heart and voice! They might even be spiritually unhealthy, but who cares? He can't transfer their unhealthy heart culture upon you unless you receive it.

We need to be mindful of three people when we receive words from others: (1) ourselves—we have the ability to say no and not receive what others say; (2) the other person—our history with the person and what we don't know; and (3) God—he will help us sort out everything we don't know or explain something that feels weird.

Have you ever had someone give you a word that didn't resonate with you? Recall the word and then ask God what "he" says about it. If it doesn't line up, does it still make you feel uncomfortable? Make sure to shake it off. There are no words that should have a lingering negative impact on you.

_____

_____

_____

_____

_____

_____

_____

_____

_____

_____

_____

_____

_____

_____

_____

_____

_____

_____

_____

_____

SEVENTY NINE

Becoming a Living Epistle

1 JOHN 3:3
*"And everyone who has this hope fixed on Him
purifies himself, just as He is pure."*

Holiness is not sinlessness; it is the ability to see what is worth protecting and then say no to sin to protect our yes to love. When we understand this, we can be the prophetic people we were designed to be without being judgmental prophets, proclaiming that people must change to inherit relationship with God. We become models and spokespersons pointing out how to get more connected to God's love. Then we can model how to stay connected by getting rid of various patterns that stop that connection and relationship.

No one needs the prophetic to point out where he or she is failing. We all know we are weak. We don't need a good shaming to get better. We need hope and life. Jesus was never motivated to use revelation to shame anyone. He was always motivated to use revelation to build a framework of heaven's heart and love for all individuals he encountered. He often spent time with people who were easy to judge, and he invited them to a place of spiritual importance through his investment in them.

Write out three ways you choose to model your relationship with God today. How will you show the world about your relationship? What would God have you do? (I would answer "as a family man", since so many ministries fail here and it's my passion, as are integrity and creativity.)

EIGHTY

Inherit Blessings

2 PETER 1:2

*"Grace and peace be multiplied to you in the
knowledge of God and of Jesus our Lord."*

One of the most beautiful parts of embracing Christ is that he
delivers us from having to reap what we have sown. It doesn't
mean there are no consequences for choices, but he stops vi-
cious cycles in our lives when we repent and return to him.
He cancels out even the normal order of inheriting bad mojo
from the fruit of our choices. We are not led by old rules, rules
that don't have the atonement and restoration of relationship to
God in their theologies. We are healed, restored, forgiven, and
blessed.

It's like the story of the prodigal son—God is waiting for us to
return and, as a loving father, he is ready to fully allow us to inherit blessings instead of reap more bad consequences from the
mistakes in our lives. Because of the redemptive nature of God,
we are poised to inherit blessings from God and not curses, if
we choose to receive them.

Is there anything in your life you've found difficult to believe could be redeemed by God? Could you make a choice today to hand the redeeming process over to him, your loving Father? Ask him about this area, pray about it, and write out what you hear.

_____
_____
_____
_____
_____
_____
_____
_____
_____
_____
_____
_____
_____
_____
_____
_____
_____
_____
_____
_____
_____

EIGHTY ONE

Gospel of Good News

LUKE 4:18

"The Spirit of the Lord is upon Me, because He anointed Me to preach the gospel to the poor. He has sent Me to proclaim release to the captives, and recovery of sight to the blind, to set free those who are oppressed."

When we begin to discern God's heart and not just the injustice in the world, we live past our generation's eyes and see with God's vision. We see what God wants to do. We see who he is and what he is doing, and we call our community into it. We have to call forth what is in God's heart as though it is fully available now, instead of looking at what's missing.

We have to discern both good and evil but live in the good, the right, and the noble. We have to keep our eyes and affections fixed on God and see things from his heavenly perspective, living from the place of his presence and heart of love. We are often at war with his perspective, and the prophetic can either compound that war or bring hope. The Bible is often called the gospel of good news! Prophecy should reflect that.

*On a scale of 1–10, ten being the best, how would
you rate the message of good news that you proclaim
every day? On a daily basis, how positive are
you about what God is doing? Stuck? Ask God to
remind you about what message he wants to drive
you with every day.*

EIGHTY TWO

God Will Go Outside Our Boxes

JOHN 1:1–3

"In the beginning was the Word, and the Word was with God, and the Word was God. He was in the beginning with God. All things came into being through Him, and apart from Him nothing came into being that has come into being."

We somehow have the narcissistic idea in the church that we are the voice of God, that we are the source for people to hear God, and if we don't speak, he will never be heard. God himself is the one who is speaking through creation, through people, through industries, through Hollywood, and more. Many times he speaks through sources a Christian would have run from (in love), e.g., a video game, an Internet article, or a political platform.

God is bigger than us, and although he uses the church and his people as his main spokespersons, he is not limited to us. In the Old Testament, God not only used Israelites to speak to the world around them, but he also used the world around them to save Israel and help Israel. This shows that God will move on his own behalf and love outside our boxes.

Ask God to show you one way he wants to use you that you would never imagine. Write down what you hear.

_____
_____
_____
_____
_____
_____
_____
_____
_____
_____
_____
_____
_____
_____
_____
_____
_____
_____
_____
_____
_____
_____
_____
_____

EIGHTY THREE

Prophecy Is About Relationship

JEREMIAH 29:13
*"You will seek Me and find Me when you search for
Me with all your heart."*

Prophecy is about relationship. No two relationships are alike, and no one can teach you exactly how to be extremely intimate with God in the specific way you long for; but relational skills can be built. He has promised you his Holy Spirit to take you on this journey.

The beauty of the prophetic is that it makes the deep things of God common. It doesn't withhold information. Most cults build their strength by knowledge brokering, or by a few holding the powerful secrets over the many. In Christianity, God has freely spoken the most precious secrets to people who don't even believe in him, because our power is in relationship, not in knowledge or secret agendas. He uses the least of these to help encourage the masses, and he is not into elitism. He reveals his secrets to humanity because he treats us all as friends.

How do you see God uniquely speak to you? Write about it. If you get stuck, write a story of how God spoke to you and compare it to other stories you have heard. How is it unique to what you know of other people's experiences?

EIGHTY FOUR

Expect the Unexpected

EXODUS 33:14
"And He said, 'My presence shall go with you, and I will give you rest.'"

God is going to show up even when you aren't in the optimal frame of mind or mood to team up with him. When you are a Christian, God is not dependent on you being in the right frame of mind to talk to people around you. You have asked God to come into your life, partner with you, and work through you. You have agreed that God can do whatever he wants through you. That means that even on the most normal, mundane days, he can be an awesome God in the midst of normality.

God wants to be present in a manifest way in our normal day. It is one of God's biggest gifts to us to manifest his presence in the here and now. We just need to learn how to invite him in or how to recognize when he is already here. We have to start believing he is actively engaged in our lives already, and we simply need to identify what he is already doing and then partner with it.

Has God ever asked you to do something or speak to someone when you weren't in the mood? What was it like and how did it turn out?

_____

_____

_____

_____

_____

_____

_____

_____

_____

_____

_____

_____

_____

_____

_____

_____

_____

_____

_____

_____

_____

_____

_____

_____

EIGHTY FIVE

Learning About the Father

JOHN 15:15

*"No longer do I call you slaves, for the slave does not
know what his master is doing; but I have called
you friends, for all things that I have heard from
My Father I have made known to you."*

We have a God who doesn't want to be listened to as a boss
or leader. He wants to be known by his heart, personality, and
Spirit. He created mankind for companionship, and many of
the ways he speaks was and will be through parables—stories,
signs, pictures, and impressions. These are as foreign as tongues
to us until we understand them. This is deliberate on his part so
that we have to seek his heart to know his mind until we have
grown in interpreting what God is trying to tell us and then
share it.

Part of the Father's joy is in developing us and then watching
us be strong and make great, very real choices. We get caught
up asking for healing gifts to heal diseases like cancer, which is
noble; but when we come into our full identity, we will also encourage sons and daughters who want to be scientists and pray
that God would empower them with a creative heart and with
faith that believes they can cure cancer.

Write down your ten favorite things about God the Father. Then tell him what they are in a relational way, the way you would tell a closest friend these things, and receive his love in return. This is a great practice to do often.

EIGHTY SIX

Interpreting God

ISAIAH 46:9–10

"Remember the former things long past, for I am God, and there is no other; I am God, and there is no one like Me, declaring the end from the beginning, and from ancient times things which have not been done, saying, 'My purpose will be established, and I will accomplish all My good pleasure.'"

Immigrants who learned English in their native countries find out their knowledge of vocabulary and grammar rules isn't always helpful in the U.S. Once here, they find they also have to learn the local slang and cultural nuances around them, not just the words, to understand and be understood. In trying to hear God, we also have to interpret or translate his words, much like a foreign language interpreter for the UN. We are sent from his kingdom culture with its relational nuances, speaking his spiritual language to the people who need to really understand who he is.

You cannot translate what you do not know or understand, and the type of knowing we are talking about is not knowledge based; it's heart based. You are translating the culture of heaven and the heart of the Father. If you want to grow, then get to know his heart culture. Look at all the ways he is talking to you. Study history. Find out how he has spoken into church movements in the past.

*What is your favorite way you've seen God speak?
Maybe it hasn't been in your own life but in the life
of someone else or a church or a movement. What do
you love about seeing God speak to people this way?
Try to see God in current popular culture right now.
Practicing this will cause you to see a whole new
level of God.*

_____

_____

_____

_____

_____

_____

_____

_____

_____

_____

_____

_____

_____

_____

_____

_____

_____

_____

_____

EIGHTY SEVEN

God Continues to Share

1 THESSALONIANS 2:13

"For this reason we also constantly thank God that when you received the word of God which you heard from us, you accepted it not as the word of men, but for what it really is, the word of God, which also performs its work in you who believe."

God never just speaks once. As a matter of fact, ask anyone who has ever heard the voice from heaven if they would mind if he never spoke again, and you will get a resounding *no!* God is eternal, and he starts sentences in the beginning of our lives that he finishes in later years. He is constantly weaving his prophetic message through circumstances and through our history, as he has done throughout biblical history.

God is sharing himself relationally with us for a bigger picture of connection, so we should listen for his voice to create more connection with him, not to just solve current problems or get what we want or need. So much prayer is self-centered and can even be selfish—it's all about what we need for now with no forethought for developing our relationship with God, his heart, and his love for us. He wants to share with us every day, not to just be around to fix something, but to walk with us.

182

Create a list of the major milestones in your life. Where was God in all of these? Can you see him weaving together a story you're still in the middle of?

EIGHTY EIGHT

Power of His Nature

1 JOHN 2:27

"As for you, the anointing which you received from
Him abides in you, and you have no need for anyone
to teach you; but as His anointing teaches you about
all things, and is true and is not a lie, and just as it
has taught you, you abide in Him."

God longs to give us the power of his nature. He promised us his anointing. This is not just an electrical, metaphysical energy that will come on us; it is a person, the Holy Spirit who dwells in us and speaks to us from a source—the Father in heaven.

In modern times, the power of God portrayed by the church has not usually been displayed in its relational context, unlike the original Hebrew understanding of it. The whole Hebrew mindset is nothing like the Western or Greek mindset that much of our philosophy (in at least the Western church) comes from. The Hebrew mindset dictates that the power of God is his very nature manifested through his presence or connection to us. It's not a live wire of current or spiritual electricity; it's his love nature and the manifestation of his personhood.

Ask the Holy Spirit to be your mentor and trainer in hearing God's voice. Ask him to teach you how to read the Bible with understanding. Write down anything you hear about this here.

EIGHTY NINE

Prophetic Attitude

1 THESSALONIANS 5:11

*"Therefore encourage one another and build up one
another, just as you also are doing."*

A prophetic attitude is birthed by people seeking to bless what
God is doing on the earth. People who grow in the prophetic
the quickest are the people who are already naturally encouraging everyone around them. Their hearts are quick to connect
with God's design in others, call it out, and help it grow.

This is how a healthy prophetic attitude starts—we get used
to building people around us. We get accustomed to being en-
couragers. Where it gets powerful, though, is not in the compli-
menting of people's nice white teeth. The power of God man-
ifests when we take on the attitude of Paul (as in Colossians):
"Do you know how I feel right now, and will feel until Christ's
life becomes visible in your lives? Like a mother in the pain of
childbirth" (Colossians 4:19). Something begins to inspire you
when you see the world around you through God's heart for it.

Make a list of all the things you see God doing on the earth right now. Even in some of the toughest situations, where is God?

_____

_____

_____

_____

_____

_____

_____

_____

_____

_____

_____

_____

_____

_____

_____

_____

_____

_____

_____

_____

_____

_____

_____

_____

_____

NINETY

Developing Life Skills

DEUTERONOMY 1:29–31

"Then I said to you, 'Do not be shocked, nor fear them. The Lord your God who goes before you will Himself fight on your behalf, just as He did for you in Egypt before your eyes, and in the wilderness where you saw how the Lord your God carried you, just as a man carries his son, in all the way which you have walked until you came to this place.'"

I love the current move of life coaching, because fathering should feel like developing life skills and empowering heart choices, not just creating boundaries. The more we grow in confidence to live from God's nature, the less we will even ask for directional words. They won't be our go-to anymore when we have to make decisions. We will always include God, but we will understand it is his joy to allow us to make powerful decisions. We will also be open to him when he does intervene, because we know he is a good Father.

Often, Christians like to come across as experts on any subject, even if they are not educated or connected to the subject, because they fear not having control more than being willing to risk in love. To have true power in relationship to those around us, we have to understand emotional intelligence and practice self-awareness. The more mature we become in love, the more we depend on prayer and our connection with people versus our conversations with them.

Has there ever been a decision you've made when God let you decide? Reflect on how that felt. How did you feel? Empowered? Scared? What was the outcome?

_____
_____
_____
_____
_____
_____
_____
_____
_____
_____
_____
_____
_____
_____
_____
_____
_____
_____
_____
_____
_____
_____
_____
_____
_____

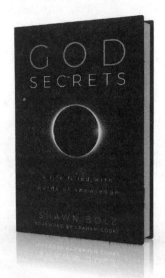

G O D
S E C R E T S
a life filled with words of knowledge

YOU CAN KNOW THE SECRETS OF GOD

AND USE THAT KNOWLEDGE TO TRANSFORM THE WORLD AROUND YOU!

Shawn Bolz shares his stories, thoughts, and biblical understanding to give you the keys to access the secrets of God.

People are paying millions of dollars for information and understanding on matters like business, economics, and politics. God has the answers, and He has made His secrets discoverable to every seeking believer in a close relationship with Him. In *GOD SECRETS*, you'll learn how to:

- Gain access to God's deep knowledge and wisdom
- Share God's mindset
- Inspire and empower others with God's thoughts and dreams
- Use words of knowledge in everyday life scenarios
- Connect with His love for all of His creation, which includes you

God's secrets are shared through words of knowledge, one of His most misunderstood revelatory gifts. Journey with Shawn as he lays out this gift in a relatable way, and gain a fresh perspective on God's direction for your business, your household, and your worldview.

GOD WANTS YOU TO DISCOVER HIS SECRETS. IT WILL CHANGE YOU AND THE WORLD AROUND YOU.

WWW.BOLZMINISTRIES.COM

G O D
S E C R E T S
WORKBOOK
a life filled with
words of knowledge

GOD HAS COUNTLESS THOUGHTS TOWARDS YOU AND THOSE AROUND YOU!
IT'S TIME TO ACTIVATE YOUR WORD OF KNOWLEDGE GIFT!

This biblically based workbook was designed to be an activity and discussion guide to help you get the most out of Shawn Bolz's book, God Secrets: A Life Filled with Words of Knowledge. Take a journey with Shawn as he gives you practical wisdom and knowledge of how to make Words of Knowledge easily accessible to YOU!

Start understanding and implementing Words of Knowledge in your daily life through powerful stories, engaging activations, and thought provoking questions. Track your progress and understanding with fun quizzes!

As an Individual or Group you will learn how to:

- Place importance on intimacy with the Lord when going after words of knowledge
- Understand the role of personal identity when giving words of knowledge
- Develop a system of accountability with God Secrets
- Practice taking risks in daily life to culture a lifestyle of words of knowledge
- Become a good receiver of God's words
- Share words of knowledge in an impactful and purposeful way

WWW.BOLZMINISTRIES.COM

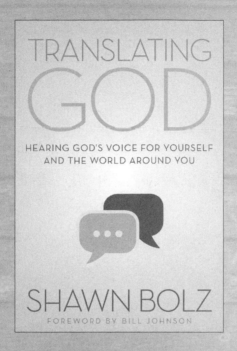

TRANSLATING GOD

www.TranslatingGod.com

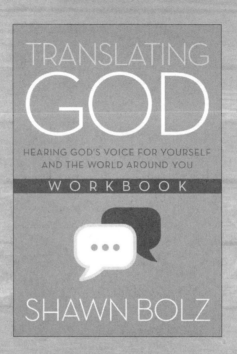

TRANSLATING GOD WORKBOOK

Be activated by Shawn's inspirational stories and use the activations, questions, and forms he includes in this life-altering workbook to chart your progress. Either individually or in a group, learn how to:

Develope your relationship with God and others.

Receive and understand revelation.

Intentionally develop and nurture your prophetic ability.

Become the fullness of God's expression of love through his revelation and voice.

www.TranslatingGod.com

GROWING UP WITH GOD
Chapter Book

Join Lucas and Maria and friends on their everyday adventures in friendship with God!

Lucas knows God talks to him, but he would have never imagined that he would hear such a specific thing about his year . . . and could Maria really have heard God about her destiny? They both have to wonder if God speaks to kids this way. Over the months that follow, God begins to connect them to other kids that grow into friends. Who could have guessed that by the end of the year, their lives would be so exciting!

Award-winning illustrator Lamont Hunt illustrates the rich, vibrant God journey of kids you can relate to. By best-selling author Shawn Bolz.

Growing Up with God is an amazing adventure!

growingupwithgod.com

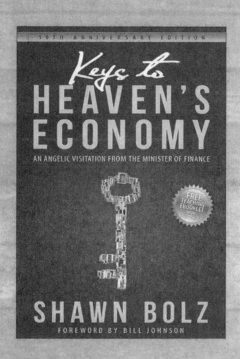

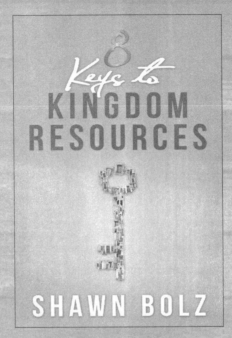

8 KEYS TO KINGDOM RESOURCES

Do you need Heaven's financial resources to see everything God has promised come to fruition? God created economics and resources to work best within the wisdom of his governing principles, and he will spare no expense at giving Jesus his reward through you. Us the foundational keys in this book to:

Value love's expression through finance,

Bring your life into alignment with Heaven's economic strategy and perspective,

Gather the resources you need to fulfill your destiny, and

Further the kingdom and shape the world.

Finances and resources help us to father the world back into God's heart. Let's do this already!

www.BolzMinistries.com